THE HERALD DIARY

A Dam Good Laugh

THE HERALD DIARY

A Dam Good Laugh

Lorne Jackson

BLACK & WHITE PUBLISHING

First published in the UK in 2022 by
Black & White Publishing Ltd
Nautical House, 104 Commercial Street, Edinburgh, EH6 6NF

A division of Bonnier Books UK
4th Floor, Victoria House, Bloomsbury Square, London, WC1B 4DA
Owned by Bonnier Books
Sveavägen 56, Stockholm, Sweden

The publisher has made every reasonable effort to contact copyright holders
of images in the picture section. Any errors are inadvertent and anyone who
for any reason has not been contacted is invited to write to the publisher so
that a full acknowledgement can be made in subsequent editions of this work.

A CIP catalogue record for this book is available from the British Library.

ISBN: 978 1 78530 420 0

1 3 5 7 9 10 8 6 4 2

Typeset by Iolaire Typesetting, Newtonmore
Printed and bound in Great Britain by Clays Ltd, Elcograf S.p.A.

www.blackandwhitepublishing.com

Contents

Introduction

IN the early days of 2022 the Crown jewels were stolen.

The Herald Diary team's commiserations naturally went to Nicola Sturgeon, for we realised that she'd no longer be able to borrow a diamond-encrusted tiara from Buckingham Palace when she eventually crowned herself Queen Nic the First of Scotiaville.

We were later relieved to discover that the genuine royal bling remained safe and sound. It was only the replicas used in a Netflix show, *The Crown*, which went AWOL.

Nevertheless, with treasure-hunting pilferers on the prowl, the readers of this book will naturally be demanding assurances that the Diary's cache of humorous tales are stored in a safe place.

Fear not!

We employ a burly security guard, who goes by the name Slightly Stroppy Steve, to keep them under lock and key.

If anyone should attempt to nab our treasures, he promises to get slightly stroppy and tear the fiendish thief limb from limb. (We wouldn't like to see Steve when he's REALLY miffed.)

Luckily for us, Steve granted us permission to borrow the best tales from the past year – originally appearing in our popular *Herald* newspaper column – in order that we could publish them in this book.

So prepare yourself for stories of waffling politicians, woolly mammoths, giant spiders, knights in clanking armour, sassy celebs...plus a year's supply of wondrous witticisms from our talented contributors.

Just make sure not to take too long reading the following yarns.

Or Slightly Stroppy Steve will be wanting a quiet word in your soon-to-be-shredded lughole...

1

24-Hour Party People

"IT'S my party and I'll be fly if I want to ..." could be a favourite song belted out by a certain blond-haired former resident of Downing Street.

The nation expects its Prime Minister to be a mover and a shaker. But early in 2022, Boris Johnson admitted to Parliament that he was more of a groover and a schmoozer, partying with politico pals in his back garden while the rest of the country was in lockdown.

BoJo wasn't forgiven for his antics. His popularity dipped precipitously, and – spoiler alert – he lost his job later in the year.

Which is why the Diary is hesitant to admit that we also enjoyed a lockdown bash. Quite a few, in fact.

Though our partying only took place on paper. In our daily *Herald* column we attempted to lighten the mood of the times by providing amusing and memorable stories.

We didn't ask our contributors to bring a bottle. Just their wit, plus a tale or two.

The tasty hors d'oeuvres served up in the following chapter recall the bodged BoJo era of government, plus other failed experiments in political science...

THE news that Scotland is to trial a four-day working week without any wage reduction doesn't impress Jarvis Fisher, who points out that an even more radical idea is being implemented in England.

He says: "From what I hear of life in Number 10 Downing Street, Boris Johnson is personally trialling a zero-day working week, without loss of pay."

MASOCHISTIC Bob Belshaw has been watching the Labour Party Conference on telly, even though there's more exciting options on other channels, such as adverts for Stannah Stairlifts on STV.

Pummelled by the pontificating politicos, Bob is now regretting his reckless decision to show an interest in the affairs of his nation.

"I once took my son to the first Star Wars trilogy, playing back-to-back at a local cinema," says Bob. "It didn't last as long as Keir Starmer's keynote ramble. Plus Keir's speech didn't have any exploding Death Stars, talking robots or lightsaber duels. What a rip-off."

IN the above tale we critiqued Keir Starmer's performance as Labour leader, concluding that he comes up short by not coming up short.

In other words, his speeches are as pithy as a Tolstoy novel, though without the amorous antics of Anna Karenina to keep things sassy.

Adding to Starmer's difficulties, Gordon Fisher from Stewarton informs us that he will never vote Labour again.

Our reader explains: "I spent the best part of thirty years as a teacher of English, drumming into young heads the rule 'i before e, except after c'. Now along comes this man – 'Keir' – breaking those rules! How can we trust such a rebel?"

THE Scots are a poetic lot who have produced many of the world's finest bards, including Robert Burns, Robert Burns and – now, who was that other chap? – oh, yes, Robert Burns.

In the spirit of the above rabble of Rabs, the Diary has decided to publish verse written by our contributors, such as the following ode by Gavin Weir from Ochiltree, which is about a blasé bloke called Boris . . .

> Oor Boris aye needs a wee hol
> So he's orf to the Costa del Sol
> A luxurious gaff, to pay would be naff
> But please, no photographs
> And if you're a prole, remember to crawl.

ANOTHER poem for our troubled times from Bearsden bard Donald Caskie:

> There was a poor man called Boris
> Forced to drive a second-hand Morris.
> In the post-Brexit Age
> He now earns a high wage
> Driving Heavy Goods lorries.

EARLIER in this chapter we evaluated Keir Starmer's Labour Party conference speech, concluding that it was a tad long, and that the initial three hours could easily have been cut.

(Along with the middle three hours.)

(And the final three hours.)

A week after Keir didn't quite smash it, it was the

Conservative Party's turn to have a knees-up. Sorry, serious political discussion.

Reader Nicholas Phillips predicted Boris Johnson's conference speech . . .

"Boris begins by saying 'Umm' followed by 'Ahhh,'" guesses Nicholas.

"This formula is repeated several hundred times while Boris swipes his hair from his forehead into increasingly phantasmagorical shapes. He concludes with a triumphant 'Umm' while the dazzled audience rises as one to reward him with a half-hour standing ovation."

THE row between the UK and France about post-Brexit fishing rights has resulted in various ministers and officials getting involved in talks to resolve the matter.

Diary reader John Mulholland was left wondering what the fish themselves think about the situation. He didn't have long to ponder, as he spotted a newspaper headline which stated: "Sturgeon Wades into French Fishing Fight."

"Nominative determinism at its best," says John approvingly. "I hope the Finns don't get involved."

YET again a Diary correspondent has sharpened his quill, consulted the muse, then supplied us with lines of verse. This ode to the odious chaps who rule Britannia was written by Jim Dunlop from Largs.

> Hail puddin' o' the UK race
> Wi' floppy mop and sonsie face,
> Presidin' o'er the House of Sleaze
> Breaking laws and lying with ease.
>
> Eton chaps are splendid blokes
> Born tae rule o'er common folks.
> Their rule of life, that greed is good
> Tae hell wi' folk that have nae food.
>
> Bring back the Empire, rule the waves,
> A wealth built on the work of slaves.
> But for those men abusin' pow'r
> A judgement when their time is o'er.

THE Diary is a staunch admirer of our nation's formidable PM. Only Boris Johnson has the intellectual daring to deliver a speech to prominent business leaders about children's cartoon character Peppa Pig. A lesser politician wouldn't have strayed from the topic of financial affairs, dispensing with the piggy pontificating entirely.

Alas, reader Dan Briggs is disappointed with BoJo. "I thought Brexit was about securing our national borders," points out Dan. "Yet Boris seems to have engineered a fleeting visit to Peppa Pig World without the use of a passport or border checks. So much for taking back control."

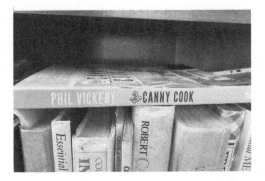

WE pointed out that Boris is a modern-day renaissance man. Not content to dabble in Ancient Greek culture, he now allows his genius to flourish by mastering the intricacies of Peppa Pig lore.

Reader Margaret Jenkins wasn't surprised to learn that our wise leader has a predilection for all things porcine. "Boris delivers his speeches in a hammy manner," points out Margaret. "He also makes a pig's ear of government policy. A rasher fellow you couldn't possibly meet."

BORIS has always been a humble fellow. Which explains why he decided to reveal in another speech that he believes he is a lot like Moses.

Scottish crime writer Douglas Skelton has been doing some intrepid detective work, and discovered that the comparison may not be entirely accurate.

Says Douglas of Boris: "He didn't part any seas because he can't even part his hair."

POLITICIAN Stella Creasy has been criticised for bringing her baby into the House of Commons debating chamber.

Reader Lisa Taylor agrees with the decision. "Relentless drooling, temper tantrums and waa-waa noises can be very irritating," she points out. "I really don't see why a baby should have to put up with it."

A FRIEND informed George Dale from Beith that a contestant on *The Great British Bake Off* had made an Eton Mess. "I was disappointed to miss the programme as I've always wanted to learn how to bake one," says George. "So I googled Eton Mess, and all I got was 'Current UK Government.'"

THE Diary continues its mission to pillory our politicos with poesy. Gavin Weir writes in with this tale of fiendish impropriety at Number 10 Downing Street . . .

'Tis the season to be jolly,
Wi' grub, balloons and a fu' drinks trolley.
But when the country gets locked down,
It causes us tae moan and frown,
As Boris acts as the Xmas clown.

A HELPFUL tip from reader Brian Wadham regarding how to understand political events that shape our great nation: "1603. Scotland's James VI becomes James I in England . . . the Union of the Crowns.

"1707. Scottish/English Parliament is formed . . . The Union of the Clowns."

DEFENDING the PM's 2020 Christmas shindig, reader Steve Young says: "Don't be too harsh. Boris definitely stayed inside his bubble. He just happens to have a bubble the size of planet earth."

WITH the furore continuing over Downing Street's lockdown Christmas party, Edinburgh comedy legend Rory Bremner contributes his theory regarding what happened: "If there was a p*** up at Number 10 last Christmas it's very unlikely Boris organised it," he says. "Because, well, you know."

AFTER a worrying amount of cocaine residue was discovered at Westminster, reader Brian Chrystal asks: "Do we now know what a 'three-line whip' really means?"

OUR discussion about the (alleged) Christmas party in Downing Street reminds reader Doug Maughan of the line from comedy great Barry Cryer, who observed that politicians are like nappies. They should be changed frequently. And for the same reason.

WE occasionally attempt to understand the majestic mind of the Scottish nation's glorious leader by taking a sneaky peek at the books on Nicola Sturgeon's nightstand. One of the novels she perused this year was *O Caledonia* by Elspeth Barker, which is about a stolid, stubborn young woman trapped within the suffocating confines of an eccentric Scottish family.

Could the reading of this book be a cry for help from an embattled First Minister who has perhaps been chained to her political family for far too long?

Perish the thought . . .

THE notoriously nosey Diary continues burrowing inside the beatific brainbox of our sanctified leader by perusing the weighty tomes stacked on Nicola Sturgeon's nightstand.

One of the books she's been reading is *The Trick Is to Keep Breathing*, which turns out to be a novel by respected Scottish author Janice Galloway.

Philistines that we are, the Diary initially assumed it was referencing covid policy, and was an instruction manual for dealing with the difficulties of wearing a claggy cotton face-mask on a crowded train.

THE future may be Orange, but the past is draped in a pattern that is definitely tartan. For the divided tribes of Alba like nothing better than to doggedly re-enact historical skirmishes, with that perennial favourite devo-max being debated (yet) again.

Not unduly delighted about this state of affairs, reader Brian Gregory says: "Gie's a break. I'm still getting my head round Pepsi Max."

PLENTY of quality quips at Michael Gove's expense after the unfortunate Levelling Up secretary found himself trapped in a BBC elevator for thirty minutes.

Gove, who is renowned as an affable Aberdonian, joked that the Beeb's staff had "successfully levelled me up".

Meanwhile, Diary reader Margaret Macdonald says: "Well, he always has been one of the strongest advocates of lockdown policy . . ."

BORIS continues to be buffeted by accusations of buffet-ing.

The evidence is damning, with an email sent prior to one lockdown event requesting attendees bring a bottle.

Reader Alan Edmondson rushes to our beleaguered PM's

defence, saying: "At least nobody can blame Boris for being involved in that aspect of the shenanigans. There's no way he'd agree to bring his own booze unless there was a prior arrangement for Tory doners to supply him with plonk from Oddbins."

YOU can always tell when Diary readers are *really* furious. They start writing poetry.

Stevie Campbell from Hamilton is incandescent with rage about the garden-based galivanting indulged in by our political overlords while the rest of the nation was in lockdown.

He also finds himself with quill in hand, an ink pot on his writing desk, and the muse looking expectantly over his shoulder.

All of which is a rather long-winded way of saying that Stevie composed the following verse for us . . .

How many lying Tories can meet,
In an English country garden,
Prime Minister don't care, if he gets spotted there,
He will simply beg your pardon.

MORE lines of verse, this time from Bishopbriggs poet Larry Cheyne . . .

There was a PM called Boris
Of very questionable mores
He stood by his chums
Even though they were bums
But now he must know where the door is.

DISCUSSING his political party on Newsnight with Kirsty Wark, the limp and languid Tory toff Jacob Rees-Mogg proved he's more venomous than he looks by calling Conservative leader in Scotland Douglas Ross: "A lightweight figure."

This stinging rebuke elicited that most Scottish of words from interviewer Kirsty, who let slip a shocked: "Ooft!"

Diary reader Bob Jamieson is more than a mite miffed with Mogg, and retaliates splendidly by saying: "At least Mr Ross doesn't bear a passing resemblance to Walter the Softy from the *Beano*."

Ooft, indeed.

IN July 2022 we hear rumours that a certain tousle-haired master of bluster and buffoonery is frantically polishing his CV, adding exaggerations, distortions and fantastical fibs. In other words, BoJo is about to be booted out of Number 10.

A friend of reader David Donaldson speculates that Mr Johnson will be elevated to the other House, where he'll be grandly titled . . . Lord Huboris.

OUR inside info proves to be correct. BoJo is vanquished, and Liz Truss becomes the hot tip to be next Tory leader. Reader Oliver Richards chuckles: "It'll be fascinating to watch robotic Truss face stilted Starmer across the despatch box. Like two Daleks having a lovers' tiff."

RISHI Sunak, also jousting for the top job, is asked in an interview if he will spend a decent amount of time in Scotland if he becomes PM.

He responds by boasting that he has been spotted numerous times in . . . Darlington.

SNP strategist and geography whiz Ross Colquhoun pedantically points out that Darlington isn't in Scotland. Using a map, compass, magnifying glass and ruler, the Diary calculates that it's actually in a location that goes by the name of England. (You may have heard of the place.)

Meanwhile, Ross says hopefully: "Unless Westminster wishes to cede land down to Darlington to Scotland?"

CYNICAL Hugh Clark from Milngavie says that if a certain Ms Truss had an extra "t" at the end of her surname our nation would have the perfect example of nominative determinism.

"WHY is Boris Johnson like April?" asks reader Jennifer Hines. "Because he didn't last as long as May."

IN August 2022, the Conservative Party find themselves leaderless, rudderless and clueless how to progress onwards. Not ideal when there's a fuel crisis on the way.

Luckily the Tories have their two inspiring candidates ready to replace BoJo. Though Glasgow comedian Mark Nelson admits he isn't impressed when they conduct a policy debate on TV.

"So glad Truss and Sunak are focusing on China," says Mark. "It will be all I'll be thinking about when I'm setting fire to my own clothes to keep warm this winter."

2

The Fundamental Importance of a Twa-Slice Toaster

BABIES are exceedingly boring, as any parent will testify. They can't tap dance, play the bongos or entertain you with an amusing anecdote. Yet people continue to fill their houses with the things.

Who knows why?

Perhaps babies are viewed as lush ornamentation to add colour and vibrancy to a house, complementing one's Dresden China figurine and that swanky ceramic vase from the Potteries.

The only problem with this theory is that babies tend to break one's Dresden China figurine and that swanky ceramic vase from the Potteries.

Then they do unspeakable things to the living room carpet.

This year one ingenious American couple seemed to have stumbled upon the perfect use for a little 'un.

They allowed their six-month-old to jet ski solo on a lake,

then posted pictures of the accomplishment on social media.

Some fuming fuddy-duddies complained that this was reckless. Though as the following tales prove, it isn't only jet skiing babies who live life on the wild side . . .

DO we detect a note of despondency in the words of Glasgow SNP councillor Mhairi Hunter, who recently visited the Co-op in Shawlands. "All is changed, changed utterly," she sighs, adding, "If you want to see hordes of people wandering round in complete bewilderment you should pay a visit."

How dreadful is the carnage, you may wonder.

Brace yourself, gentle reader, for Mhairi reveals: "The hummus is in a different place."

A HEART-WARMING tale about the joys of friendship. Reader Gordon McRae tells us of two old pals who were enjoying a modest libation in a hostelry.

One turned to the other and said: "After I'm dead and they're putting my coffin in the grave, will you pour a bottle of whisky over it?"

"No problem," said his chum, "but do you mind if it passes through my kidneys first?"

ON social media the delights of the Glasgow Subway are celebrated. "Part of the appeal is feeling like you're rattling around in an old Lucozade bottle at the bottom of a bin," enthuses one devotee.

AN occasion made awkward by inappropriate musical accompaniment.

Tony Griffin from Aberdeenshire recalls the DJ who was broadcasting his show on a Scottish radio station one evening when news broke of the death of Fred Astaire. At the following commercial break the jockey legged it downstairs to the station library and grabbed the first Fred Astaire record he could find.

Making it back to his studio just in time, he slapped the disc on the turntable and breathlessly announced: "This is a tribute to Fred Astaire, who died today – 'Dancing Cheek to Cheek.'" The record started playing: "Heaven, I'm in heaven . . ."

MORE inappropriate musical accompaniment. A hospital-ised reader was taken to church in a wheelchair, along with several other patients, all in the same condition.

The organist thought it appropriate to play "Stand Up, Stand Up for Jesus".

Alas, none of the congregants could.

STUDENT Richard Taylor was in a bar with a pal who slugged eight pints of snakebite & black, which is – as the mixologists amongst our readership will know – a blend of lager, cider and blackcurrant cordial.

Feeling queasy by night's end, this poor fellow groaned: "Think I'm gonnie puke. Must be something wrong with that blackcurrant cordial."

OUR readers often go out on a limb for a story. Some go out with a brace of limbs. Fraser Kelly recalls being a student nurse in the Western Infirmary and attending a double below-knee amputation.

Afterwards he was ordered to change into civilian clothes and return to the operating theatre, whereupon he was handed two large yellow bags, containing the legs.

He was told to take them to the Gardiner Institute of Medicine, which at the time meant leaving via the casualty main entrance and turning right, down Great Western Road.

Strolling along the street carrying his gruesome package, Fraser spied a police patrol heading towards him.

At which point he realised he might have some explaining to do . . .

Luckily Strathclyde's finest sauntered by without a word, and Fraser legged it to his destination.

THE local pigeons of Glasgow's Central Station are not a source of delight for the vast majority of exhausted commuters, who usually dismiss them as feathered vagabonds. Reader Ted Burt overheard a young English girl with a different opinion.

Standing in the station with her father, she pointed to a bird hopping past with a half-eaten sandwich in its beak. In a cut-glass accent, sounding very much like a miniature Audrey Hepburn, she trilled: "Dad, isn't that a handsome looking pigeon? Isn't it impressive?"

The father, perhaps more world-weary than his daughter, merely replied: "Looks like your average sort of pigeon to me."

THE above story reminds Russell Smith from Largs of the tale of the homing pigeon that was late back.
"It was such a nice day, he decided to walk," says Russell.

OFFICE politics can be complicated. A reader tells us her favourite colleague is the water cooler in the corridor.
"It always does its job, never complains, never gossips," says our reader. "Unfortunately I can't say that about anyone else I work with."

STROLLING in Glasgow's West End, author Deedee Cuddihy overhead a chap in his thirties talking on his phone:

"If we all had crystal balls, Ian, we'd be able to make that decision up front. But we don't," said this fellow.

"I couldn't help wondering if crystal balls is some kind of 'man condition,'" says a concerned Deedee.

TO the Edinburgh Festival, where reader Kirk Owen spies a chap on the cobbled, cosmopolitan streets tossing in the air various knives, axes and other pointy objects, all of which are liable to give a fellow more than just a paper cut.

The knife-thrower is no mere litter lout, for he insists on catching the objects, too.

It transpires that he is a street performer, and our reader is impressed when the chap introduces himself to the gathering crowd by roaring: "Make way for . . . The Mighty Darren!"

Says Kirk: "I guess he had no choice but to become a daredevil juggler, especially when his Christian and middle names happen to be 'The' and 'Mighty'. On the other hand, 'Darren' sounds like the name of a spotty youth handing out chicken drumsticks at KFC."

STANDING in a late-night taxi queue, reader Veronica Rushton overheard two scantily clad debutantes chatting.

One of the girls glanced down at the top she was wearing, or not quite wearing.

"D'ye hink I'm overflowin' a wee bit much?" she said, referring to her décolletage, much of which was on display.

The other girl scrutinized the area referred to for some time, then said: "Overflowin'? Niagara Falls is a drippin' tap compared tae you, doll."

FOOD-LOVING reader Jennifer Robinson says: "I've never understood how Snow White was nearly killed by something as uninspiring as an apple. To bump me off, you'd have to poison a profiterole."

"I WISH Medusa would stop objectifying people," says reader Neil Black.

ANOTHER Edinburgh yarn. George Edwards from Motherwell took his young grandson to our capital city to see the sights.

The only sight the cultured lad was interested in seeing was an ice-cream van.

Such a vehicle was found, and two ice-creams purchased . . . for a cost of just under ten pounds.

"I can't wait till my grandson's old enough to drink," sighs George. "Taking him down the pub for a heavy sesh will be cheaper."

HARD-WORKING Russell Smith from Largs recalls his student days, when he had a holiday job as a temporary postman.

"It was better than walking the streets," says Russell.

VISITING a bustling hostelry in Aberdeen, reader Andy Wright overheard the following conversation between two young chaps . . .

CHAP 1: Mandy's a lovely lass, ken? But I don't see much o' a future for us. See, she only has a twa-slice toaster in her flat.

CHAP 2: And . . . ?

CHAP 1: Well, I like four slices for ma breakfast. So I need a four-slice toaster.

CHAP 2: Can't you just toast twa slices o' bread? Then, when you're finished, toast another twa?

CHAP 1: (Aghast) But that'd mean waitin' fur ma second twa slices!

CHAP 2: Aye, sorry. Wisnae thinkin'.

IRATE scientists and angry members of the clergy often get in touch with the Diary and demand to know why we so rarely discuss the metaphysical tensions that exist between the worlds of faith and science. Let it never be said that we have deliberately dodged a profound or controversial topic.

So, in the spirit of open-mindedness and philosophical enquiry, we quote reader Jason Watkins, who says: "A Higgs boson particle walks into a church. The priest asks it to leave. The boson says, 'But without me, how can you have mass?'"

ONCE more the Diary dares to tackle the most contentious questions of our age, with Eric Arbuckle from Largs demanding to know: "If one enjoys a jam sandwich whilst wearing a sleeveless jacket, would this be a gilet piece?"

INAPPROPRIATE musical accompaniment, continued . . . Tom Bradshaw from Bellshill recalls a wedding reception where the father of the bride insisted on hearing a rousing rendition of the popular song "Let's Call The Whole Thing Off".

Luckily this prickly paternal advice was ignored, and the newlyweds continued being newly wed.

WE pointed out that enjoying a jam sandwich while wearing a sleeveless jacket could be called a "gilet piece".

Eric Arbuckle from Largs notes that a "Gigli piece" is enjoying a jam sandwich while listening to an operatic aria sung by an Italian tenor (forename Beniamino).

A FINAL example of inappropriate musical accompaniment. A reader was on the phone to an insurance company, and had been put on hold, when the song "Little Lies" by Fleetwood Mac came on, with its memorable lyrics: "Tell me lies, tell me sweet little lies . . ."

"I wasn't convinced of the wisdom of that advice," says our reader.

3

The Savage Goldfish

A FEW months ago the Diary was devastated to hear rumours that pop band Little Mix were on the verge of splitting up.

For those who don't follow the music scene, Little Mix are a modern day version of the Beatles. If all the Beatles had been named Ringo. And Ringo hadn't bothered to learn drums.

Some of our more suspicious readers may fear that, like Little Mix, the Diary team will call it quits one day.

We categorically assure you that this will never happen. For our editorial staff manage to avoid falling out with each other by never talking to each other in the first place.

Meanwhile, our talented roster of story contributors are prevented from leaving our employ as we keep them locked in a dungeon secreted deep within the catacombs of Diary Towers.

Which might seem a tad cruel. Though it's for a good cause. For if they weren't chained to a mildewed stone wall, while being fed one slice of mouldy bread a day, they couldn't possibly have provided us with the following delightful tales . . .

ENERGETIC Diary correspondent Laura Hodgson took her thirteen-year-old granddaughter for a vigorous ramble to the summit of Arthur's Seat. Whilst marching, Laura related the history of the famous Edinburgh landmark, explaining that some scholars believe the site's curious name refers to King Arthur, that feisty fellow who owned a jabby, stabby hunk of metal called Excalibur.

"So it's named after an imaginary character?" said Laura's granddaughter. "If those are the rules, it might as well be called Bugs Bunny's Seat."

SEARCHING in the kitchen for something tasty to drink, the husband of reader Janet Allinson stumbled upon a bottle of tomato sauce in the fridge.

"I could put a straw in this and drink it, I suppose," he said to her, adding: "After all, tomatoes are a fruit. Which makes this a fruit smoothie."

OUR readers were sad to learn that Strathclyde Uni's legendary student union is moving from its long term home of 90 John Street. Those "ten floors of fun" were a rite of passage for many a sozzled scholar.

Ken Bailey recalls ending a night there with a flatmate who became rather hysterical on the wobbly walk home.

"Jeezo, I've got the hiccups," slurred this booze-addled chap.

"Don't sweat it," said Ken. "It's only hiccups."

"Yeah, but what if they're terminal hiccups?" shuddered the chum.

THE Diary is scornful of those who skip through life in a frivolous and carefree manner. We prefer to march down the road of enlightenment in a never-ending quest for knowledge and wisdom.

As does reader Bill Conway, who says: "In my life I've always been a follower of the Greek philosopher Mediocrates, who famously said: 'Meh . . . good enough.'"

THE triumphs of youth are but fleeting, claims Gordon Fisher from Stewarton. The other day he shook his head despondently while complaining to his wife that he longs for the glory days when he wrote humorous material for STV.

Gordon's missus looked at him with pride, then exclaimed: "Wow! All these years, and I didn't know you'd been a comedy writer for our national independent television station."

"Oh yes," said Gordon, revelling in the sort of smug satisfaction that is only ever experienced by an author revered in his own lifetime. "I had several jokes read out by Glen Michael on *Cartoon Cavalcade.*"

CHECKING the North Lanarkshire Leisure website for updated information, Gerry McElroy from Cumbernauld came across the following message from the Time Capsule in Coatbridge: "As well as a change to our booking system, showers will now be operational, and there will be no limits on spectating numbers."

The Diary was aware that there are many energetic activities to be enjoyed in North Lanarkshire, though we didn't realise that splashing around in hot, soapy water – while starkers – is now a spectator sport in those parts.

WE continue recalling the glories of Strathclyde Uni's student union. Rod Trimble once attempted to chat up a fellow student in the bar. He assumed he was coming across rather favourably until the girl pointed to one of the bouncers by the door and informed Rod that this burly chap was her boyfriend.

Rod nervously glanced at the bouncer.

"Don't worry," said the girl. "He won't be jealous. He knows I'm only into good looking guys."

"I'VE got this habit of continually correcting people's grammar," admits Ian Noble from Carstairs village, though he's trying to cut down.

The other day he told a colleague off for using "went" instead of "gone".

She responded in exasperation: "Why are you so dogmatic?"

"I think you mean pedantic," said Ian.

THE grandmother of reader Tony Grant won a decent amount of dosh on the lottery. Tony wondered if she would mark the occasion by booking a slap-up lunch with chums.

"Not me," said Gran. "I'll just do a wee celebratory hoover round the living room."

THE glories of Strathclyde Uni's student union, continued. Reader Patricia McDonald walked past the building with a work colleague, who said: "I met my wife in there. We've now got three children, which means shelling out on toys, clothes, food and expensive summer vacations."

Emitting a world-weary sigh, he added: "Wish I'd never entered that building. Turned out worse for me than having Bernie Madoff as my financial adviser."

UNESCO, the United Nations Cultural Body, have revealed there's no threat of Edinburgh losing its world heritage status, even though critics have complained about the city's "Disneyfication".

Edinburgh native Alan Baxter says: "If UNESCO are really unconcerned about the evolution of Edinburgh, perhaps we could get away with a few more subtle changes. For starters, how about replacing that stone monstrosity at the top of the Royal Mile with a bouncy castle?"

CHILDREN'S picture book *The Tiger Who Came to Tea* has come under fire from a Scottish charity for "reinforcing gender inequality" because the story includes a stay-at-home mum and a father who goes out to work.

Reader Brenda Moir believes all classic children's literature should be updated, starting with the oeuvre of Roald Dahl.

"That man was responsible for millions of rotting teeth," says Brenda. "Which is why his most famous book should be rewritten as *Charlie and the Gluten-Free Salad Bar*."

MEDICAL musings from reader Daniel Fletcher, who says: "The heart is such a strong muscle because it's constantly pumping iron."

THE various members of Edinburgh's Carnethy Hill Running Club managed to bag all of Scotland's Munros in a single day, which is an incredible achievement.

Though not according to reader Bruce Johnson.

"Big deal," he shrugs. "Yesterday I managed to bag all my shopping in under a minute."

THE perils of marriage often include dealing with a partner who snores. The wife of reader Bert Thomas decided to get separate beds to escape the niggles of hubby's nocturnal nasal noiseathon.

Though she later reversed her decision.

"Couldn't spend a night without me?" said Bert, smugly.

"It's not that," his wife replied. "I just hate the idea of dealing with two unmade beds every morning."

WHEN reader Tricia Fulford was an undergraduate at St Andrews University she shared a flat with a posh girl from London, named Daisy.

Daisy had plenty of spending cash, courtesy of her generous parents, and she never prepared a meal for herself, preferring to dine out for breakfast, lunch and dinner.

Once, our reader attempted to persuade Daisy to try cooking for herself.

Daisy responded by devising the following list, which she later hung in the kitchen, as a reminder to herself of the advantages and disadvantages of such a radical policy.

Pros & Cons of Cooking Food
Pros: Food.
Cons: Cooking.

(Daisy never did get around to preparing her own meals.)

SCOTLAND'S reputation as the world's fine-dining capital has been boosted by a Bellshill eatery's introduction of a delicacy called the rice and curry meat roll. Essentially it's a massive deep fried ball, packed with chicken, rice and curry sauce.

Reader Craig Johnson suggests our nation shouldn't rest on its laurels after such a culinary triumph.

"Isn't it time we stopped being coy about our favourite passion?" he says. "Let's cover our entire land mass, from the Borders to John O' Groats, in a layer of crispy batter."

RELAXING with his wife in an Edinburgh wine bar, reader Ted Plimpton overheard a couple at a nearby table arguing.

The woman ordered a bottle of wine, leading her chap to suggest that they'd both had enough vino already.

"Well," said the lady, as the cork was pulled, "you're always telling me not to bottle things up . . ."

WE continue updating children's books to be more woke. Reader Mike Bennet suggests a certain C.S. Lewis classic should be re-titled: *The Lion, the Woman With Alternative, Though Perfectly Acceptable Pagan Religious Beliefs and the Wardrobe.*

CURIOUS Stevie Campbell from Hamilton wonders if it's true that when students at Glasgow School of Art approached the board asking for information about the future of the fire-damaged building they were told to: "Draw their own conclusions."

THE wife of reader Rob Linford claims he's greedy. To prove her wrong he's taking her out for tea and biscuits.

"It's bound to be a special day," says Rob. "She's never given blood before."

WE continue updating classic children's books to appease woke idealogues. Laura Minter believes Jack London's ripping yarn, *White Fang* – which describes the adventures of a savage wolfdog – is too triggering for modern youth.

"The story should be rewritten so that it's about a savage goldfish who can't be tamed," says Laura, "until it's accidentally flushed down a toilet."

HARDWORKING Jenny McLean cooked her teenage son a three-course meal, washed up, then asked the lad if he could possibly dry the dishes.

"Why do I have to do EVERYTHING round here?" he groaned, in a self-sacrificing sort of manner.

VISITING Warwick Castle with his wife, reader Len Young spotted some peacocks wandering in the castle grounds. One bird didn't look too sprightly, and was dragging its once resplendent tail along the grass.

"I think someone's needing powdered Viagra rubbed in his feathers," commiserated Len's wife.

CUNNING Linda Brennan from Paisley waited for the cover of darkness before sneaking out of her house carrying a refuse sack which she intended to toss in a neighbour's wheely bin, her own being full.

She had just reached her destination, and was lifting the

bin's plastic lid, when a neighbour walked out of her front door, also carrying rubbish.

From the neighbour's outraged face it was clear that she realised what dastardly deed was about to take place.

Though her look of indignation rapidly dissolved, and she started to laugh.

"I was just about to dump my rubbish in YOUR bin," she admitted. "We're obviously as evil as each other."

WHEN Ralph Bentley from Croy was a child, his father grew his own vegetables. The busy chap also cooked lunch for the family every Sunday, always serving his prized veg, which he never washed properly.

Oftentimes a creepy-crawly would be discovered by a knife or fork while the food was being munched.

If a complaint was made, Ralph's dad would say: "Shhh! Keep schtum, or everyone will be wanting one."

POPULAR 1990s sitcom *Friends* is playing on Netflix, and reader Donna Embery is watching it with her teenage daughter, Bella, who thoroughly approves of the show, and not just because of its entertainment value.

"It's a fascinating history lesson," Bella told her mum. "Now I know how people lived in olden times."

WE'VE decided to figure out how our readers can become immortal, so they can delight in the Diary for all eternity.

Gerry MacKenzie has a cunning idea, though he points out that it involves a lot of bad luck along the way.

"Start breaking mirrors," says Gerry. "For every twenty you smash, you'll live 140 hideous years."

OUR tale about the horrors of discovering a creepy-crawly on your plate of food inspires Malcolm Macintyre from Lesmahagow to get in touch to point out that there is something far worse:

"Finding half a creepy-crawly on your plate."

A TALE of whoops, woe and wit from reader Mungo Henning, who spotted an elderly chap in a Glasgow shop carrying a large number of purchases.

Unfortunately the poor fellow tripped on his way out the door, resulting in a painful, sprawling fall.

Luckily a young police officer also happened to be leaving the shop, and rushed to the old fellow's aid.

As the prone pensioner piteously moaned in agony, the policeman was keen to discover the extent of his injuries.

"Can I get you an ambulance?" he asked.

With deadpan stoicism of the patented Glesga brand, the old man replied: "Ah widney hiv oanywhere tae keep it, son."

A TALE of healthcare and hostelries. Christopher Ide from East Renfrewshire tells us of a registered medical practitioner who strolls into a bar and asks for a daiquiri cocktail. The barman mixes the ingredients and sprinkles grated hickory into the drink.

Handing it over, he says: "Here's your hickory daiquiri, doc."

THE Diary continues updating children's fiction to placate woke idealogues. Lisa Allen is tired of Mary Poppins being portrayed in such a stereotypical female fashion as a nanny.

"She should be rewritten as a plumber," says our reader. "One who gets great satisfaction from ramming her magic umbrella down U-bends to unblock toilets."

WE continue trying to figure out how our readers can become immortal. David Reading suggests anyone interested in the life eternal should visit the Scottish Parliament to listen to the speeches.

"You may not live forever," says David. "Though it'll sure feel like it."

4

Polish for Beginners

THE contest to crown a new leader of the Conservative Party – who would also get a wee shotty at being Prime Minister – got underway in July 2022.

In the lead from the beginning was hingmy, closely followed by what's his name.

Though the Diary much preferred sure-we've-seen-her-face-before.

They were a charismatic bunch, all right. Each one ready to strut the world stage like Churchill. (The growly wee bulldog from the insurance ads. Not the bloke with the cigar.)

These head boys and head girls of the true-blue brigade all strived to give their platitudes some attitude; to win the country over with cliché-ridden claptrap. (Or was it claptrap-ridden clichés? We were never entirely sure.)

Unfortunately none of the front-runners and ropey ranters

desperate to be PM proved to be as memorable and magisterial as the tales in the following chapter . . .

POO TIN

BOXING fan Jimmy Sitwell worked in an Aberdeen gym, helping to train young fighters. One teenage scrapper was awarded the seemingly impressive nickname of "The Horseshoe".

One might imagine this was because he packed a powerful punch, making his opponents feel like they had been whacked on the jaw by a boxing glove packed with a solid hunk of blacksmith's metal.

This was not the case, says Jimmy, who explains: "When this young bloke got knocked down – which was often – he curled up, whimpering, on the canvas, making him look like your average horseshoe."

WHILE Sarah Peel was clearing out rubbish in her loft, she stumbled upon old pop magazines from the 1970s. Flicking through one mag, she came across a missive in the letters page comparing Scotland's Bay City Rollers to the Beatles.

This letter grandly and authoritatively opined: "The Tartan Five are definitely better than the Fab Four. The Rollers are talented, good-looking and have great personalities. What more can you ask?"

Our reader was impressed by this knowledgeable comment, and says: "I'm now searching my old magazines to see if I can find a letter claiming Sydney Devine was better than Johnny Cash."

BROWSING in a charity shop, reader Gordon Murray spotted an ancient book titled: *A Guide To Surgical Procedures.* Our reader adds: "Perhaps not surprisingly the appendix was missing."

SUPERGROUP ABBA have reformed in order to record a new album. Inquisitive *Still Game* actor Sanjeev Kohli has managed to discover some more information about any possible future gigs.

"They've started rehearsing for that new ABBA concert," he reveals. "It was incredibly loud. You could hear the drums from Nando's."

MANY people are still working from home, points out reader Emma Broughton, and she has a top tip for those in this situation.

"Blowing on the wine in your mug will help to convince your Zoom meeting that your tea is hot," she says.

DETERMINED to get herself fighting fit, Lisa Copper from Whitecraigs signed on for an aerobics class at the local gym.

"I bent over, twisted around, gyrated and jumped up and down for an hour," says Lisa. "Though by the time I got my leotard on, the class was over."

VISITING his local hostelry one weekend, Christopher Oats overheard one chap at the bar say to his friend, who had downed rather a lot of pints: "You're gonnie regret all that boozin', come the mornin'."

His chum replied: "A dinnae hink so. There's no way I'm gonnie be awake till the afternoon."

IN a morbid frame of mind, reader Pete Harris has been mulling over what he wants his final words to be, as he lies on his deathbed. He's now decided on: "I left a million pounds, and it's under the . . ."

WE proudly present a dramatic vignette involving cosmetic dentistry and a Central European nation, courtesy of reader Maurice Doyle . . .

Said Maurice to his dentist: "I want my teeth whiter."

The dentist replied: "Have you tried polish?"

Said Maurice: "Chcieć moich zębów biały."
His dentist ignored him.

WE live in an increasingly health conscious era, where fit-as-
a-fiddle folk sweat it out at the local gym before going home
to pick away at a plate of – yeuch! – salad.

Reader Pam Murphy notes that even the elderly population are under the sway of the taut-n-trim ideology, as she
discovered the other day while sitting at a bus stop in Glasgow
city centre.

She overheard one old chap say to another: "The wife wis
sayin' that I should be eatin' salad, cos it's good for me. Well, I
just telt her that potatoes are a vegetable, which means a bag
o' crisps is salad."

After a pause, he added rather forlornly: "Course she wisnea havin' any o' that. I still ended up bein' force-fed a wad o' lettuce leaves."

RETIRED English teacher Martin Lee tells us that one of the books he once taught was the Arthur Miller play *Death of a Salesman*.

Not all of his students were enamoured by this modern American classic. He recalls one frustrated scholar shaking his head in disappointment when told the name of the book he'd be studying.

"What a rubbish title," harrumphed this young fellow, who added: "Nae surprises, eh? Shoulda been called: Death (Or Mibbe No') Of A Salesman."

THOUGHTFUL advice from reader Ted Edwyn, who says: "If you see someone wearing camouflage, make sure to walk right into them, so they know it's working."

MORE barfly badinage. Gareth Lloyd from Stenhousemuir was in his local watering hole when he overhead a bloke mutter to his pal: "I've become one of they multitaskers."

"Zat right?" slurred the pal.

"Yup," said the first fellow. "I can listen, ignore and forget, all at the same time."

THE husband of reader Jenny Hogan was worried that he was getting too old to party. To prove he was still young at heart, he arranged a night out with the chaps. The plan was to go boozing and carousing for at least ten hours solid. However, after a 7pm start, Jenny's hubby returned home at 9.45pm.

"We're still going to party for ten hours," he informed Jenny, before heading off to bed with a cup of cocoa. "We just decided it's best to do it in incremental shifts over the next decade."

OUR yarn about a sneaky person enjoying a sly slug of wine during a Zoom conference reminds Robin Mather from Musselburgh of the times he visited a YMCA to watch a local jazz band.

Coffee was on sale, but regrettably no alcohol. So Robin hid bottles of beer in his inside jacket pockets and smuggled them into the venue.

Having purchased a cup of coffee, and rapidly downed it, he surreptitiously poured beer into the now empty receptacle.

Though before drinking from it he would stir the booze with a teaspoon, thus completing the ingenious deception.

OUR story about the intricacies of the Polish language reminds comedy great Andy Cameron of the time his friend, an eminent optometrist from Mount Florida, had the one-time Celtic goalkeeper and Polish national Artur Borac in his chair, and asked him to read the bottom line on the wall chart.

Artur apparently said: "Read it? He was in my class at school."

A DOG'S tale. Grant MacKenzie from Bearsden recalls his uncle's border collie, Pal, who was trained to perform numerous useful tasks around the croft in Lewis.

One day our reader watched in amazement as Pal, with a hammer in his mouth, climbed up a ladder onto the roof of the house, and proudly presented the tool to his master, who was in the process of mending loose slates.

To Grant's surprise his uncle seemed annoyed. Wearily gathering up the "helpful" hound in his arms, he shouted down: "That's the third time today I've had to carry this bloody dog off the roof. He's yet to master climbing DOWN ladders."

OUR *Death of a Salesman* anecdote reminds Moira Campbell of the time she taught supply and was asked to cover a Higher French class who were reading a Maigret story. It so happened that the creator of Maigret, Georges Simenon, had died the night before, and it had been announced on the radio.

When Moira informed her class of this coincidental occurrence, one unhappy chappie said: "Could he not have died before he wrote this book – it's awful hard."

FORMER English teacher Colin Palmer worked in a school where one of the plays taught was the exceedingly grim *Men*

Should Weep by Ena Lamont Stewart, set in Glasgow during the 1930s Depression.

Colin recalls one of his young scholars saying: "No wonder it was called the Depression. Anybody would be depressed if they had to read this tripe."

WHEN she was a university student, reader Mary Browne served tables in a restaurant at weekends, an occupation she enjoyed, especially when she learned the tricks of the trade.

One of the older waitresses once told her: "Always wait until a customer's mouth is full before asking them if they're enjoying their meal. They'll be too embarrassed to do anything other than nod vigorously while trying to swallow."

PERSONAL trainer Jennifer Ross tells us that she once agreed to create an exercise regime for a high-flying female lawyer. For some reason the lawyer was particularly interested in learning to do the splits.

"Do you think you can teach me that?" she asked Jennifer.

"Well, it depends," said Jennifer. "How flexible are you?"

To which the lawyer responded: "Oh, I can do any days, except Fridays."

THERE'S a sign in the window of a small bakery on the outskirts of Dundee that reads: "Try Our Famous Iced Buns." Reader Bob Greene has often wondered what the iced buns are famous for, exactly. The silky smooth texture of their icing? The gooiness of the fillings?

Eventually Bob decided to ask, though on the day he visited the bakery, there was only a teenage boy at the till, not the usual baker.

"So why are your iced buns famous?" said Bob.

The boy mulled the question over for a long, ponderous moment, then replied: "They're like the Kardashians. Famous cos they're famous."

"Hopefully nobody puts that young fellow in charge of the shop's marketing strategy," says Bob.

MANY years ago reader Scott Hattam was watching a television documentary about one of his favourite troubadours, Paul Simon. The singer-songwriter was strumming sweetly on his guitar when Scott's young son wandered into the room and asked what sort of instrument the man on TV was playing.

"That's an acoustic guitar," said Scott. "Which means it's a guitar that doesn't use electricity."

"Oh," responded the young boy, who added: "Does that mean when we light a fire with wood, to make sausages when we go camping, we're using an acoustic cooker?"

MOST elderly folk are kept active by running after their grandkids. Though there are now plans to further amp up oldster energy levels by providing pensioners with robot dogs to walk.

Languorous reader Ted Young isn't persuaded by this plan.

"Maybe they could start me off with a robot budgie in a cage," he says. "And if that works out, I'd be delighted to be upgraded to a robot tortoise."

WHEN reader Marni McGurty found her old telephone from the 1970s in the loft, she showed it to her young grandson, who was puzzled by the instrument. "It's very clunky," he said, "and where's the screen to watch TikTok videos?"

WE mentioned a bakery near Dundee where the iced buns are famous because . . . Well, we never actually discovered why the buns are famous. Though the sign on the bakery window trumpets their celebrity. And when did a bakery window ever lie?

Meanwhile, reader Bert Tappman informs us he once holidayed in Canada, where he came across a rural food store in Nova Scotia where a sign proclaimed that you could buy: "A Nova Scotia delicacy! The best fish in Canada . . . and the World!"

"I bought the fish," says Bert. "Very nice it was, too. Though I can't say it was the first time I'd tasted this Nova Scotia delicacy, because it came in a box labelled Birds Eye Fish Fingers."

A LOVE story. Reader Malcolm Boyd was delighted when his wife mentioned how compatible they are as a couple.

Is this harmony due to the missus and Malc's sizzling romantic chemistry, which makes them very much a modern day Romeo and Juliet; an Abelard and Heloise for the ages; or even a reboot version of Mickey and Minnie?

Not quite.

Malcolm's wife proceeded to qualify her statement, explaining that while hubby can hear high frequencies, she can hear low frequencies. Therefore neither of them ever misses a ringing mobile phone or the front doorbell.

Forget the heart – lurv's about the lugs.

ESSENTIAL dietary advice from reader Gordon Casely, who says: "By replacing your morning coffee with green tea, you can lose up to 87 per cent of what little joy you still have left in your life."

DESPERATE to get fit, Madge Lindsay took a beginner's swimming class at the local gym. Another first-timer was an elderly lady bobbing next to our reader in the pool.

When the 45-minute class was over, she turned to Madge and said: "If this is swimming, I'd rather learn how to drown. At least there'd be less faffing around with the arms and legs."

WE mentioned that ABBA have reformed to record a new album. Reader Shirley Sutherland is still in awe of the combo's achievements, explaining: "ABBA are the only palindromic act to have a palindromic hit (SOS) in a palindromic genre (pop)."

FRUSTRATED reader Pat Hogan got stuck in a traffic jam the other day. He says: "I was there for so long that even the sat nav said, 'Are we there yet?'"

WE previously mentioned a rare delicacy enjoyed by a reader visiting Canada, which on further investigation turned out to be the sort of treat you can enjoy anywhere.

Reader Bob Collins recalls being a child and visiting his grandma in Shettleston every Saturday for lunch.

As a treat Gran always made what she called her 'Extra-Special Secret Recipe Steak & Kidney Pie.'

When Bob asked what the secret was, Gran whispered that it was an ancient concoction, handed down from mother to daughter over many generations.

"Then one day I caught her preparing the age-old recipe," says Bob. "She had a can opener in one hand, a Fray Bentos pie tin in the other.

"Gran thought it was hilarious. Though as far as I was concerned, the strong connection between me and Gran had been permanently Fray-ed."

5

COP Land

"HURRAH!" screeched the Diary team back in November of last year. We had just discovered that the planet was finally going to be saved. For the great, the good and the gregariously green had decided to meet up in Glasgow for COP26.

Or perhaps the situation was only going to get a whole lot worse, with the environmental talking shop producing a cloud of hot air that would hover in the sky above Scotland, before blasting a Glesga-shaped hole in the ozone layer.

Thankfully the Diary has genuine green principles. For we have created a product so darned entertaining that our readers constantly pester us to recycle material by publishing the best of our stories each year in the very book you are now holding.

The following chapter further bolsters our green credentials by celebrating COP26, the Save Our Planet jamboree to top 'em all . . .

POLITICALLY-MINDED Alan Ward has been hearing rather a lot about some sort of bigwig shindig to take place in the West of Scotland.

Our astute reader says: "All this talk about COP26 must mean they're filming the next movie in the Police Academy franchise in Glasgow. Personally I'm thrilled. I've always been a huge Steve Guttenberg fan."

YOUTHFUL Swedish activist Greta Thunberg has scandalised Scotland by suggesting our noble country may not be a world leader when it comes to climate change.

Clearly it's time for decisive action, meaning Scottish Greens leader Patrick Harvie must change greetin' Greta's mind by inviting her to inspect the prize-winning marrows in his allotment.

Meanwhile, talkRADIO presenter Julia Hartley-Brewer gallops to the defence of our beleaguered nation, stating: "I don't regard Greta Thunberg as a world leader on any topic except truanting."

WITH thousands of delegates coming to Glasgow for COP26, Charles Murray from Newton Mearns believes that the ever helpful Diary should provide suggestions for what newcomers to the city can do to entertain themselves of an evening.

Charles gets the ball rolling with the following topsy-turvy advice: "Why not catch the Underground to West Street,

where you'll find the liveliest bars and restaurants in the . . .
South Side."

WE continue suggesting entertaining destinations for the
visiting COP26 gang. Joe Bailey says they should saunter over
to Glasgow's Victorian graveyard, the Necropolis.

He adds: "Being surrounded by tombstones will remind
the delegates about all the climate-change pledges they are
about to make, which are quickly buried when they think the
public's forgotten."

LIKE an ageing Hollywood starlet who goes under the scalpel
in order to acquire a more youthful visage, Glasgow has been
receiving an intense sprucing up.

The Diary has no idea why this nip and tuck is taking place, though surely it's merely coincidental that COP26 is happening at roughly the same time.

Glancing out his office window overlooking Broomielaw, Dougie Jardine was astonished to spot a nearby path being buffed up. No expense had been spared, for two street-sweepers were working on the job.

Though unfortunately they had only one brush and pan between them.

WITH COP26 underway, the mischievous chaps at the BBC's *Off The Ball* radio show asked listeners a question. If they could give a COP delegate a taste of Scotland, what is the one delicacy they would offer?

This led one culinary-minded fellow to suggest the scrummy Hebridean treat Ceann Cropaig, which is a fish head stuffed with oats and liver.

The Diary thinks this sounds delicious. Though does it truly represent our nation's sophisticated eating habits?

It's not even deep-fried.

SCOTTISH comedian Mark Nelson says: "The advantage of COP26 being in Glasgow is that world leaders get an immediate glimpse at what an apocalyptic world would look like."

A VICTIM of the ghastly Scottish weather, reader Nancy Barker says: "Couldn't climate change activists in Glasgow demand less money is spent on windmills and more on umbrellas?"

BOASTFUL reader Dan Featherstone reveals he has a degree in climate change.

"In ten years," he adds, "it turns into two degrees."

THE world-famous visitors to the West of Scotland have quickly settled into life in our sophisticated and cultured neck of the woods.

Greta was spotted getting to grips with the Glesga lingo in Festival Park, lustily tossing crude words into the autumnal air, and very likely scandalising the local squirrels and hedgehogs.

Meanwhile, Joe Biden's motorcade whizzed past a Greggs bakery, though disappointingly the POTUS didn't stop for a pastie. Perhaps he was maintaining his appetite until he could purchase a haggis supper from a chippy further up the road.

But what has any of this got to do with local Glasgow gyms? Rather a lot, apparently.

For Nuffield Health have stated that they: "Anticipate higher usage over the coming weeks due to COP26."

The Diary wonders why.

Could it be that Boris and Macron intend on ironing out their differences by seeing who can peddle faster in a spin class?

APPARENTLY some members of the Scottish police force are enjoying their deployment to the West End of Glasgow during COP26. Strolling along Kelvin Way, near the Art Gallery and Museum, Deedee Cuddihy engaged two officers on patrol in casual conversation.

"Are you getting fed up with folk like me stopping to chat?" she asked.

"Not at all," one of them replied. "I normally work in an area where most members of the public would be very unlikely to approach the police."

"And where's that?" enquired Deedee.

"Clydebank," came the answer.

EAGLE-EYED former Labour politician Sir Brian Donohoe spotted that the registration number on the tail of the private plane bringing the Russian delegation to COP26 ended in 007.

With a raised eyebrow, Sir Brian says: "From Russia with love . . ."

THE Diary is delighted that megastar Leonardo DiCaprio has graced COP26 with his presence. Though the shindig was already a glam affair, with Boris and Nicola providing the sort of Hollywood pizzazz that hasn't been witnessed since the third *Look Who's Talking* movie.

But is Leonardo really the best person to promote the COP agenda?

After all, he's most famous for appearing in a film about a boat that could have easily reached its destination, if only global warming had got its act together faster, and melted all those pesky icebergs.

THE gathering of green-minded geezers and gals may be named COP26, but there's certainly more cops on the streets than a mere 26. This week the assembled might of the constabulary attempted to block an elderly demonstrator who was dressed rather conspicuously as a tree.

One nearby wag was heard shouting at the leaf laden chap: "Are you Special Branch?"

OBSERVANT Richard Broomhall spotted a procession of climate change protestors carrying a silver birch tree along Buchanan Street.

The group handed him a flyer explaining their campaign against the destruction of this venerable plant.

"I wonder what the flyer was made from," says Richard. "Hopefully not silver birch."

THERE have been many amusing placards carried by global warming protestors. Our favourite was one held aloft by a young lady, which read: "The planet is hotter than my boyfriend."

Bad news for the planet . . . and her boyfriend.

THE Diary considers itself the last bastion of culture in a world of fickle philistines. We provide fine art with our photographs, and philosophy, courtesy of the profound musings of our correspondents. Sometimes we even ravish our readers with poetry, such as the following ode, titled "Heroes", by Gordon Wright . . .

> Desperate Dan, now there's a man,
> Who could take a smack from a frying pan.
> Then Superman, who could run and fly,
> Swooping on villains, from the sky.
>
> Now Greta's here, the bravest by far,
> She's just said the F word to Andrew Marr.
> And a climate march is turning to farce,
> As Greta starts chanting, "Up your a**e."
>
> Eco warriors, reserved and pensive,
> Will find these sweary words offensive,
> So Greta, in case you get arrested,
> For saying words that are detested,
> Tell us quick, before they ban it,
> How on earth can we save the planet?

THE friendly Scottish welcome to weary wayfarers is famous the world over. Debbie Meehan was awaiting a train from Ayr into Glasgow when she got chatting to four young foreigners. She assured them that they were on the correct platform.

Alas, the sneaky Glasgow train then decided to depart from an entirely different platform.

Debbie's new chums turned out to be Argentinian journalists visiting the country to film a COP26 documentary.

Being the forgiving sort, they promised not to mention Debbie's dubious directions in their final cut.

STROLLING on Buchanan Street, reader Patrick Harris spotted environmental campaigners lustily singing the John Denver classic "Take Me Home, Country Road".

"Having witnessed the hypocritical behaviour of the COP26

delegates," says Patrick, "I suggested to the campaigners a more appropriate Denver song – 'Leaving on a Jet Plane.'"

AMERICAN politician Alexandria Ocasio-Cortez made plenty of new chums at COP26 by glugging an Irn-Bru, then saying something best summarised as: "Yum!"

But should the feisty left-winger from the Democratic Party have been so vocal in supporting Scotia's fizzy favourite, muses reader Bert Stroud.

"After putting up with Trump for years," he says, "you'd think she'd be allergic to anything orange."

INSPIRED by all the pontificating and protests surrounding COP26, reader Lisa Devlin asked her elderly mother what she thought about renewable energy.

Mum shrugged, and said: "I've not got an opinion on it, though your dad says he gets all the renewable energy he needs from a cabinet in the living room. That's where he keeps his bottle of Johnnie Walker."

A CLIMATE change activist glued his face to a Glasgow road during COP26, reports Iain Ferguson from Prestwick. Our curious reader wonders if the chap's face, along with the rest of his body, is still there.

"Has he been promoted to a roundabout, or at least a traffic island?" muses Iain. "And if he needs a haircut, does the barber come to him?"

6

The Diary's Resident Guru
Has His Say . . .

THE Editor of the Diary is an opinionated chap. To prevent him getting too excitable, the rest of the staff keep him manacled to a leather chair in his office, with each of us taking it in turns to read him restful lullabies throughout the day.

Occasionally we allow him to express his creative side, by providing him with scraps of paper and a crayon.

Unfortunately he tends to eat the paper while ramming the crayon up his nose. (He tells us that he likes to savour the scent of a good crayon. For him it's more rewarding than a Cuban cigar.)

On a good day he may use the writing materials to scribble a column for us, in which he expresses his thoughts and feelings about the world.

We've decided to publish a selection of these articles, because we believe they're both penetrating and profound.

Actually, that's not true. We only agreed to publish them after the Editor said that if we didn't, he would feel compelled to ram a crayon up one of our noses instead of his own.

So for the sake of free speech (and free nasal passages) here's the first of the Editor's wise messages to the nation . . .

SHHHH. Keep this to yourself. Don't let it get around. Let's make it our little secret. Just me, you and a few thousand other readers who happen to be perusing *The Herald Diary* at this very moment.

The confidence I've decided to divulge . . . (Deep breath. Calm, calm. Must be a brave little solider. Just like ripping off a plaster) . . . is that I like to play around.

Whew! There. I've admitted it. I'm promiscuous. A philanderer.

Just when I seem to have settled down, there I go again, eying the available talent. Thirsty for thrills. Hungry for what is hot and not mine.

I'm talking about football, of course.

The rule is that when you're a young whippersnapper you pick a footy team, and that's you for life, like taking a Victorian marriage vow.

You follow your guys through ups and downs, pain and sorrow, feast and famine, skill and scuff-the-ball. Who cares if the entire relationship between you and the chaps on the field is as rational as a Dali dreamscape? Love has its own logic, which is no logic at all.

At least that's how it is for everyone . . . except me.

I started out supporting Hearts. I was a kid. I didn't know any better. Besides, they were almost the local lads when I was growing up in Livingston, a new town fairly close to Edinburgh that didn't host its own top level team back then.

And what was not to like? Hearts were doing well in the league, the newspapers informed me. (I never went to a game.) And they wore those fetching plum-coloured T-shirts, or football strips, or whatever they were called.

Best of all, when I was walking home with my mates after school, I now had something to yak about once we had exhausted the topics of TV shows (*The Young Ones* versus *Monty Python*) and girls (Julie in a short tartan skirt versus Lisa in tight denims).

Things changed when Hearts lost the league and I moved to Glasgow.

In my new school there was one cheeky chubby chappie who held court at break times, like a particularly belligerent Bernard Manning. His humour was dangerous and wounding, and he had it in his power to isolate any member of the group who didn't share his views.

One of his views was that Rangers were the greatest footy team in the universe. I readily agreed. Anything for a quiet life. It appeared that I was now a diehard Gers fan.

And so I stayed.

Until uni, when I became good friends with a Celtic fan. I was understandably intrigued by his allegiance as I'd never supported a bunch of athletes in stripey T-shirts before. And the green in their kit gave them a sort of minty freshness which was most appealing.

I was sold. Even went to a match! Paid good money to bask in the body odour of a few thousand other blokes. Enjoyed a perfect view of the back of those other blokes' heads.

At one point, one of the minty-fresh fellows possibly scored. Everyone seemed chuffed, at any rate.

Since then I've broadened my scope to support Manchester United, Nottingham Forest, Aston Villa, the LA Lakers (though they may be a basketball team; I'll have to do some research) and Motherwell (definitely not basketball, though perhaps not football in its truest sense, either).

Now I've got a pressing problem. Who to support in the future?

Perhaps I'll opt for Aberdeen United. The Granite City could do with a diehard fan like me.

7

Curly (of the Wurly Kind)

SO the stripey green and white footy team won the Scottish Premiership in 2022.

Or was it the blue, non-stripey chaps who bagged the title? It was one or the other, anyway.

Isn't it always?

Scottish football isn't known for its infinite variety. It's more like opening a family-size box of Quality Street and only finding Green Triangles and Orange Crèmes.

No wonder so many Scots are losing interest in this kicky-ball cartel, and are instead turning to *The Herald Diary* for their sporting gasps, groans and golly-gosh-did-that-just-happen?!

In the following chapter you'll discover numerous feats of athletic achievement, including a pack of rats racing round Glasgow.

In another story an elderly couple in a boozer look set to

win a gold medal in grumpiness. And let's not forget the rural fellow enjoying a prize pee.

So brace yourselves, sport fans. Make sure not to spill your pie or Bovril on this page. For you wouldn't want to interrupt our glorious Diary athletes as they push themselves to the very limits of human endurance for your entertainment . . .

THE sparkling table-talk amongst the Glasgow cognoscenti currently revolves round the number of roving rodents scuttling through the city streets. If you haven't spotted a rat on its perambulations, you just haven't arrived, da'ling.

Craig Griffiths recalls growing up in the city's East End in the 1970s, when such sightings were also commonplace. One evening he was strolling to the shops with his older brother when he spotted a rat on the pavement. Our reader, being a manly little chap, shrieked.

His brother, trying to calm him down, said: "Dinnae be greetin', now. It's just a wee Glesga version of an Ozzie kangaroo. Y'know, like Skippy."

THE scene is a bar in Paisley, where reader Barry Casper spotted an elderly couple sitting in a frosty silence, which was suddenly broken by the chap, who said: "I telt you tae leave ma new teeth well alone. But anything that's mine, you've got tae huv a go, eh?"

SCIENTIFICALLY minded reader Cal Miller provides us with a handy guide to chromosomes:
  XX = Female
  XY = Male
  YYY = Delilah

THE hubby of Kate Stewart was reading about the TRNSMT music festival held in Glasgow Green. He wasn't impressed.

"When we had music shindigs in my day," he grumbled, "the organisers could always afford to splash out on a few vowels to go with the syllables."

A STORY of a conscientious worker. Reader Marc Hall asked his manager if he could leave work early. "My boss said yes, if I made up the time," says Marc. "So I said, 'Sure, it's eleventy past four.'"

A HANDY tip from reader Tony Thompson: "Change your password to 'incorrect', then if you can't quite remember it, your computer will give you a hefty hint."

A TALE from the factory floor. David Clark from Tarbolton recalls sitting at his tea break one day with a chap called Hughie, who suddenly let out a deep sigh and groaned: "Och, ah weesh tae goodness it was Friday."

This prompted another chap to respond: "Ach, Hugie, yer jist weeshin yer life away."

Without pausing for thought, Hughie replied: "Well then, ah weesh tae goodness it was last Friday."

ON a train from Glasgow to Edinburgh, reader Sophie Mulvanie overheard two young chaps in suits and ties talking.

Said one chap to the other: "If I was rich enough I'd take a hiatus from my career. But as things stand, all I can afford is the odd sickie from the office."

ANOTHER story of the working world. Reader Fay Alper once bagged a job in an office in Glasgow city centre. On her first day, a female colleague whispered to her in the hallway: "I wouldn't stay with this firm if I were you. It's a rotten place to work."

Fay enquired what was the problem. Management? Colleagues? Terms and conditions?

"The dispensing machine in the canteen only has cheese and onion crisps," said the distressed colleague. "And they're all out of date."

VISITING a hostelry in Cumbernauld, reader Frank Cash overheard one chap say to another: "I'm all for the state o' marriage. But I jist think it'd be fairer for all concerned if instead of saying 'I do' at the altar, you were allowed tae say: 'I'll gie it a shot.'"

WE mentioned a popular shindig held in Glasgow Green. Reader John Mulholland says: "When the festival was launched it was given a trendy, eye-catching name. Who could have predicted that in the era of the pandemic that name would be even more relevant? It may lack vowels, but it certainly doesn't lack irony. Hats off, then, to the person who came up with the name TRNSMT."

WARNING. Proceed with caution. The following tale involves a tragic event that may distress those who love cute animals, biscuits . . . or both.

Still with us? Then reader Bob McGuinness has a story to tell.

"I bought a pack of those animal-shaped biscuits," says Bob. "But I had to take them back. The seal was broken."

ONE of the delights of being a university fresher is that organisations are apt to toss free stuff your way. Very occasionally the free stuff can even be useful. For instance, we hear that Cathouse, the famous Glasgow rock venue, is handing out mugs at the Freshers Festival in Argyle Street.

And these aren't just any old mugs. Oh, no. For as Cathouse proudly proclaims: "These things can hold both hot AND cold liquids and it has a handle!"

(To be fair, a mug with a handle is an exotic item when located in student digs. Most students prefer to sip their liquid refreshments out of ashtrays. Sometimes they even empty the ashtrays first.)

WHILE we're on the subject of fluids. Reader Wendy McCullough unearthed from the back of a cupboard a rusty old tin of the once popular powdered milk called Marvel.

She showed it to her young granddaughter, who was most intrigued. "How do you squirt powdered milk out of a cow?" enquired the little girl.

THE daughter of Angela Thompson from Cumbernauld sat a high school English test. The teen was not delighted about the situation.

"What's the point of learning novels, plays and poetry?" she grumped. "It's the twenty-first century. I should be tested on celebrity Instagram posts."

THE ageing process explained. "When I was young I'd sneak out of the house to go to parties," says reader Belinda Murray. "Now I sneak out of parties to go to my house."

IN a cruel mood, reader Eric Hill says he has changed his name on Facebook to "No one". He adds: "Now when I see idiotic posts I can click 'like' and it will say 'No one likes this.'"

THE Diary never shies away from controversy. Though perhaps we strayed too close to contentious waters when a correspondent dared posit the theory that a person from Yorkshire is actually a southerner. At least from the perspective of a Scot.

Yorkshireman David Waters says that this sort of talk would not go down well in the White Rose county.

Furthermore, he supplies us with an alternative description of a person who hails from a certain geographical location of the British Isles.

Explains David: "My mother's definition of a southerner was someone who carves meat you can see through."

THE challenges of relieving oneself in the countryside. Reader Peter Mackay recalls the two old chaps who had been out boozing.

After consuming multiple pints they find themselves strolling – sorry, staggering – homeward through arable lands. The eldest of the chaps suddenly realises his bladder needs emptying, and he proceeds to make the necessary arrangements.

A local polis, spying him in mid-micturition, taps him firmly on the shoulder, and booms: "You can't pee here."

The old chap looks up patiently and explains, "I'm not peeing here. I'm peeing way over there," then proudly points some feet away, where his splish is splashing.

VISITING an Edinburgh café, reader Sarah Morgan heard two ladies in their twenties chatting about relationships.

"All I want is a guy who's faithful, loyal and attentive," said the first lady.

Her friend rolled her eyeballs. "That's not a man you're after," she said. "It's a basset hound."

ENLIGHTENING advice from reader Dave Nicholls, who says: "If a lamp post disappears on your street you can always pin a 'missing' message on a cat."

HAVING a tipple at the nineteenth hole of his local golf club with chums he's known for decades, reader Alan Jones proudly boasted to the gang: "Y'know, I think the years have been kind to us."

One of his chums responded: "The years were never the problem. It was the weekends that did us in."

GLANCING in the fridge, reader Barry Sullivan noticed that his wife had bought a box of milk chocolates plus a box of dark chocolates.

When Barry enquired why his wife purchased both, she responded: "You know that balanced diet I keep talking about going on? This is it."

ROISTER-DOISTERING Russell Smith from Largs points out that "Paisley" has a less innocent meaning when lurve is being discussed.

Russell tells us that a friend of his was once given a lecture on the birds and the bees by his father, where the following advice was proffered: "When you're going with a lassie, stop at Paisley. Don't go all the way to Glasgow."

The Diary is shocked to discover that Scottish locations

have ulterior erotic definitions. We're now loath to enquire what it means to pop in to Auchenshuggle . . .

A FRIEND working at the Isle of Wight Festival reminded reader Gordon McRae of an ancient conundrum.

Q: What is cream and brown and comes steaming out of Cowes?

A: The Isle of Wight ferry.

"Unfortunately changes in livery for the ferries over the years has rendered the joke a nonsense," sighs Gordon.

Not to worry. If Gordon ever finds himself in Cowes harbour in the dead of night, surreptitiously carrying tins of cream and brown paint, he can always render the joke topical once more.

MORE humour that's past its sell-by date. Finlay Buchanan from Edinburgh recalls that back in the days when Binns department store dominated Princes Street, an elderly Edinburgh lady was bemoaning the fact that she couldn't find a bra that fitted.

"Have you tried Binns?" asked her friend.

"Yes," she replied, "but they rattle when I run for the bus."

THINKING about a certain twisty-turny chocolate snack, reader John Dunlop asks a most profound question: "Has anybody ever had a Straight Wurly?"

THE Diary is renowned for its uncanny ability to identify the key issues of the day, which are analysed and debated in these pages.

For instance, mulling over the intriguing qualities of a certain twisty-turny chocolate snack, we demanded to know if anybody had ever tasted a Straight Wurly.

Inspired by this thought, reader John Dunlop asks: "Why do we put up with Old Jamaica? There should be a Brand-Spanking New Jamaica."

FOLLOWING on from our discussion about there being no Straight Wurly, only the curly kind, Bill Lindsay gets in touch to inform us of a writing exercise he gave to his Higher English class, over thirty years ago. The lesson was titled, Supermarket Semantics . . .

Fresh beef.
Fresh poultry.
Fresh fish.
Just how fresh is *dead?*

INSPIRED by our Straight Wurly debate, Gordon Casely enquires: "Why are bargain-basement stores often upstairs?"

WHEN he was a student, reader Adam Webb played bass guitar in a rock band. They auditioned for a manager who told them: "That was fine, just fine. Now all you need is decent tunes, lyrics and musicianship. Oh, and it would help if you were a bit more attractive."

"The band broke up immediately afterwards," sighs Adam. "It wasn't musical differences. It was musical similarities. We were all rubbish."

8

Bond Is Back . . . (and So Are Fuzzy Elephants)

DAVID Beckham recently revealed that his wife, Victoria, has eaten the same meal, every day, for the last twenty-five years.

It doesn't even sound like a particularly appetising dish, for there's no red meat, chips, whisky sauce, overflowing gravy-boat, goodies plucked from a deep-fat fryer, wobbly jelly with lashings of double cream, or post-prandial Cuban cigar.

The Diary team indulges in all of the above, first thing every morning. For we believe in the importance of starting the day with a healthy, invigorating breakfast.

Victoria, alas, only nibbles on grilled fish and steamed veg. Or if she's feeling particularly daring she takes a gamble on steamed fish with grilled veg. No wonder she always appears to be scowling.

Unlike picky, pouty Posh, the Diary understands that variety gives life its essential vim and vigour. This also applies to the treats we offer up to our readers.

The following chapter involves such juicy morsels as doughnuts, unicorns and woolly mammoths, all of which are delicious.

Though we advise you to go easy when it comes to scoffing your daily portion of woolly mammoth. You wouldn't want to end up with an icky hairball in your throat . . .

AN Edinburgh doughnut company is baking a range of Scottish-themed delicacies, including the Flower of Scotland, which features a saltire cross and Irn-Bru glaze.

David Donaldson is disappointed. "I looked in vain for a doughnut called the Budget," he says. "That's a doughnut covered in a jam tomorrow glaze with an unusually large hole in the middle."

OUTRAGED reader Scott Keeley says: "It's ridiculous that people let off Guy Fawkes Night fireworks in September. My cat gets so scared he runs up the Christmas tree."

ENCOURAGING news for readers who fear that today's youth are ignorant of the past glories of Western civilization.

Oliver McGarrity was watching TV with his fifteen-year-old son, when the teen piped up: "Doesn't that guy on the telly look like Hugh Hefner?"

Our reader was shocked to hear his offspring referencing the late publisher of racy magazines such as *Playboy*, and enquired how the youngster had heard of him.

"Every kid at my school knows the Hef," beamed the boy. "Dude was a total legend."

Oliver tells the Diary: "My son's never heard of Hamlet, Mozart or Newton, yet he reveres 'the Hef'. I'll have to visit his school to ask what exactly is being prioritised on the curriculum."

NERVOUS reader Jenny Barrett says: "My biggest fear about becoming a zombie is all that shuffling about. Shouldn't an exhausted zombie be allowed to hail a taxi, once in a while?"

WE mentioned an Edinburgh doughnut company is baking Scottish-themed delicacies. Reader Tony Lynn wonders if they will make an Independence Referendum doughnut. "You eat one and decide it's not for you," he says. "Then someone from the SNP turns up and says: 'C'mon, have another. And another. Keep chewing till you swallow what we're offering."

THINKING about drinking, reader Stan Crowcroft says: "If you don't like tea then a cup of tea is not your cup of tea."

WE are told by a reader that a former director of a House of Fraser store had the habit of rearranging the layout of the departments.

One employee, when asked by a customer where the men's department was, is reported to have answered: "I don't know, madam. But if you just wait at the escalator, you'll see it going past."

PSYCHEDELIC musings from Neil Moore, who points out: "Reading a book is just staring at a dead piece of wood for hours and hallucinating."

ENCOURAGING news. Researchers have found evidence that scoffing cheese and cream may ward off heart disease.

Jim Borland from Largs is delighted with this counterintuitive revelation, and says: "I'm now looking forward to researchers discovering that the best way to train for an Olympic gold is sitting on a couch inhaling a family-sized bag of spicy Doritos. Hand me my medal now."

ONE of the presents Carol Cooper's husband bought for her fortieth birthday was a helium inflated balloon, designed to look like a pink unicorn.

Which was a pleasant surprise. Until it broke free from the string and weight mooring it, and floated to the high ceiling in the living room, where it hovered like a perky, pink cloud for the next few days, constantly reminding Carol that she was forty.

Eventually our reader could take no more of this torture. Sellotaping a sewing needle to the end of a broom, she marched off to have a joust with the mythical beast.

An action that distressed Carol's six-year-old daughter, who wailed: "Mummy! It's cruel to stab a unicorn!"

"I stabbed it anyway," chuckles our heartless reader. "It's high time that pink unicorns were put on the extinction list."

MATHS teacher John Perkins once found himself glancing over the shoulder of a pupil who was hunched at his desk, struggling to complete a set of problems.

John pointed to one calculation in the lad's jotter and said: "You've made a schoolboy error, there."

The youth looked up at his teacher with a pained expression on his face.

"I am a schoolboy," he said. "Surely that's the sort of error I should be making."

THE sixteen-year-old son of reader Susan Roche had a Friday and Monday off school, though he was meant to use the time to prepare for some fast-approaching tests. This led to the following conversation between pestering mum and incalcitrant youth.

Pestering Mum: Did you do any work today?
Incalcitrant Youth: Yeah. Haircut.
Pestering Mum: Getting a haircut's not work.
Incalcitrant youth: Totally is. My fringe is gone. Now I'll be able to see my test papers.

WITH the hullaballoo surrounding the release of new James Bond flick, *No Time to Die*, reader Eddy Cavin attempts to predict the newspaper and TV coverage that is sure to arise . . .

• Bond Is Back! (Note that exclamation mark. No other chap warrants as many exclamation marks as James B.)

- Who Was the Best Bond? (George Lazenby, no doubt about it.)
- Bond Girls . . . Then and Now. (Marvel as women who were in their twenties some fifty years ago, now – gasp! – look considerably older.)
- STV broadcast all the Bond films in sequence. (Though perhaps missing out that weird 1960s version of *Casino Royale*, featuring Woody Allen. It would be too cruel to force an unsuspecting population to watch that again.)
- News channels demand to know . . . Who Will Replace Daniel Craig!? (The Diary hopes it will be Woody Allen. Everyone deserves a second chance.)

DECIDING to teach his grandson about the wonders of literature, reader Ralph Johnston took the little chap to the local library.

Once there, they got talking to the head librarian, who explained the function of the venerable institution she presided over.

To Ralph's grandson, she said: "Just think of us as a 3D version of the Internet, minus the cute cat photos."

A TALE of sin and redemption. Sandy and Jock emerge from the Kirk, where the meenister has delivered a real hellfire and damnation sermon on the Ten Commandments.

The pair trudge along in silence, until Sandy finally confesses: "Weel, Jock, at least I've nivvir made a graven image."

THE husband of Pam Jones told her about an article he read in a science magazine, which revealed that boffins are close to discovering a way to bring woolly mammoths back from extinction.

Said hubby to Pam: "I wonder if they'll be farmed, like sheep?"

He then added with a delighted grin: "Now I know what I want from you for Christmas. Woolly mammoth mittens, with matching socks."

THE granddaughter of reader May Potter has been learning in primary school about the origins of certain surnames. For example, she now knows that the ancestor of someone called Cooper would most likely be a barrel maker, because such a tradesman is referred to as a "cooper".

This got May's granddaughter thinking about her own surname.

After mulling it over for a while, she asked Gran: "Do we have the surname Potter because our ancestors liked to potter around?"

FUN with Fido. Reader Roderick Archibald Young tells us that his mother bought one of those ball-throwing gadgets many dog walkers now use. "She says she can hurl the ball over 500 metres," says Roderick. "But I think that's a bit far-fetched."

OUR revelation that the woolly mammoth could be brought back from extinction thrills reader Sarah Atkinson. "I've wanted another pet since my last one died," she says. "But will a woolly mammoth fit in my hamster cage?"

OUR yarn about the Ten Commandments has one reader suggesting a more precise definition for one of them . . .

Thou shalt not commit adultery = You can't have your Kate and Edith.

FOR his son's birthday, reader Nick Ronaldson bought him an alarm clock that swears instead of bleeping. "He's in for a rude awakening," says Nick.

WE continue devising modern-day uses for woolly mammoths. "If we breed them in Scotland, we could put one in goal for the national footy team," suggests Alex Campbell.

"They're not especially limber, and have limited tactical awareness. But since they're about six times the size of the goal, none of that should matter."

THE above suggestion is not taken seriously by reader Adam Lennox, who scoffs at such a foolhardy plan.

"Woolly mammoths are incredibly hairy, and the next World Cup is in boiling hot Qatar," he points out. "To have any chance of winning the competition, we would have to give our goalkeeper a full body wax."

(Luckily Scotland didn't qualify for that particular competition, so we never had to book an appointment at the beauty parlour.)

KEIR STARMER'S latest wise pronouncement is that the next James Bond should be female. David Donaldson is not impressed, and says: "How come there isn't a clamour for Harrison Ford to step down and let a woman take the lead in the next big blockbuster ... *Indiana Jane and the Roots of Darkness*."

WE continue pondering the cultural impact of the smoulderingly suave superspy with the licence to be a lothario.

Iain Harrison from Linlithgow informs us that he once suggested to a lady of his acquaintance that he could easily be the next James Bond.

"More like the new Columbo," was her response.

"Needless to say, the relationship did not survive," sighs Iain.

MORE musings about everyone's favourite hirsute and hefty hulks . . .

"The original mammoths lived during the Ice Age," points out Tom Ogilvy, "meaning they probably excelled at winter sports. So they should represent the UK at the next Winter Olympics."

Is there any specific activity our reader would like to see them compete in?

"I've never followed the Winter Olympics," admits Tom. "So I don't know the individual events. But it would be truly inspiring if the woolly wonders arrived back in Britain with medals swinging from their tusks after grabbing gold for being the world's best at snowball fighting."

9

Rictus Grins, Spatter Patter and Other Celebrity Shenanigans

THE Loch Ness Monster has traditionally been a shy sort of celeb. She doesn't post on Twitter or Instagram, refuses to star in her own reality TV show, and has no interest in becoming this week's most discussed social influencer.

Some people may criticise Nessie for preferring a lonely loch to an LA swimming pool. Yet that tendency to shun is also part of the fun. It maintains her mystery and allure.

Though no longer.

For she's been on the move, and was spotted earlier this year lolling in a lake in London's Wimbledon Park.

Perhaps she was training for the popular tennis tournament held in those parts, and is now desperate for the fame and fortune that arrive with the trophy.

Nessie's jaunt to a London suburb proves conclusively that

celebs are a fickle tribe; the only constant in their lives is a craving for attention.

Which we have agreed to lavish on them in the following chapter, which shines a Diary spotlight on the many achievements and wise pronouncements of our nation's favourite actors, artists, singers, writers and comedians . . .

ROCK stars rarely have detailed retirement plans. Rather than move to Bournemouth, or take up crown bowls, your average lead singer or guitarist prefers to die young, a rictus grin smeared across his face as he is slowly crushed to death beneath a writhing Ben Nevis of amiable groupies.

Not Justin Currie.

The lead singer with Glasgow band Del Amitri knows exactly how he'll spend his twilight years, having stumbled upon a shabby shed in a field, which he plans on converting into a swingin' local night spot.

"I'm going to retire here and sell whisky through the window," enthuses Justin, though he has strict stipulations regarding what punters will be allowed to purchase.

"No timewasters," he growls. "And you get what you're given."

Justin charitably adds that he might allow ice on the premises, though patrons will have to bring it themselves. They'll also have to fetch water, if they desire it, from a nearby pond.

(Somehow we don't think Justin's business plan will be giving Wetherspoons owner Tim Martin any sleepless nights . . .)

AN education in the brutal arts, courtesy of Glasgow crime scribe, Denise Mina, who reveals that she met a retired police surgeon the other day and "He wants everyone to know this: It's blood SPATTER not SPLATTER".

(For further clarification, the Diary feels dutybound to point out that the phrase "that pure gied me the boak" is the correct medical terminology for the layman to use when stumbling upon blood spatter. Or splatter, for that matter.)

DENISE Mina, continued. When the popular writer isn't yakking to the police about blood patterns, she manages to find time to scribble on scraps of paper. Having done rather a lot of that, recently, she has now completed her latest magnum opus, and is feeling rather blasé about the experience, revealing she'll be: "Air-punching, bursting into song, ruffling the hair of passing street urchins and patting dogs all day."

Blimey.

We wonder how she reacts after completing something really important, like a Sudoku puzzle.

BOASTFUL River City star Sanjeev Kohli says: "I've just bought a block of Cathedral cheese SO big that my fridge has been given city status."

IT'S lucky that Fife comedian Richard Pulsford is a talented stand-up, because his attempts to change career have sadly come to naught.

"I've received a rejection letter from NASA," says Richard. "Strangely, it says there's no space on their training programme."

SCOTTISH actor and star of TV show *Outlander* Grant O'Rourke is feeling a tad confused about our baffling countryside. "People who climb big hills in Scotland: when are you peeing?" he asks. "Do you just hold it in till you get back down? Or do you pee off the top? What if it's windy?"

AUTHOR Kathleen Jamie has been appointed Scotland's new national poet, or Makar as it's called in these parts.

Stevie Campbell from Hamilton wonders if there's any truth to the rumour that the runner-up for the position was a chap called Owen Pye.

Stevie says he heard that the panel eventually decided that it just didn't have the stomach for Makar Ownie Pye.

THE Diary team occasionally tackles the major topical issues of the day. For instance, we often debate whether the earth is flat, or some other shape entirely. (Spoiler alert: after exhaustive research, we've come to the thrilling conclusion that it's . . . flat. Probably.)

Another favourite subject, Marmite: scrummy or scuzzy?

Glasgow comedian and panto favourite Johnny Mac has issued his opinion on this contentious subject, saying: "Just tried Marmite for the first time . . . NEVER AGAIN. It was like licking the inside of a farmer's welly boot."

GLASGOW crime writer Douglas Skelton has revealed that in his future creative endeavours he will be blending fantasy fiction with his love of a good mystery.

"I'm planning a set of stories set in Middle Earth in which a well-known character with a dual personality dons a rain-coat, smokes a cigar and solves crimes," he says. "It will be called Gollumbo."

THE above story inspired Gordon Campbell from Crieff to devise another mash-up between the world of fantasy and crime.

He says: "If the late, great Mark McManus's Taggart had turned up in Middle Earth, would he have been able to sneak in the line, 'There's been a Mordor?'"

TWO shocking announcements from Edinburgh crime writer Ian Rankin, who admits . . .

a) He's rubbish at Cluedo. (What next, we wonder. Is Stephen King about to reveal he hates Halloween?)

b) He doesn't know who the killer is when he begins a novel, only figuring it out after he has progressed deep into the narrative.

Which has the Diary speculating whether other great writers have worked this way. Perhaps Herman Melville reached page 927 of Moby-Dick and said: "Hmm. It might be rather intriguing if I introduced some sort of aquatic species into the story. Maybe a tadpole?"

THE story above has us speculating whether other famous authors have improvised without much forward planning.

Reader Sandy Morrow wonders if Irvine Welsh got three quarters of the way into *Trainspotting* before deciding to start from the beginning.

He suddenly realised that his hard-hitting tale about Edinburgh blokes addicted to Milk Chocolate Hobnobs was never going to top the bestsellers list.

COMEDIAN Simon Evans spots that the Glasgow Hilton have named their meeting rooms after Scottish rivers. "Can't help feeling they've missed a trick, though," he says, noting that "Forth" is the name of room . . . five.

THE Diary likes to inspire its staff members by practising what we call the carrot-and-stick method of motivation. In other words, we hit our minions with carrots and force feed them sticks.

Apparently this isn't the only way to get things done in an office, for we hear that STV are searching for new employees for their flagship *Scotland Tonight* show.

Anchorman John MacKay explains what's required. "Do you have a sharp mind, good ideas, and can you pour a good Scotch?" he asks.

An intriguing job description, though we wonder if it complies with current trends for diversity in the workplace.

We sincerely hope that prospective employees who can merely pour a refreshing bottle of Buckfast will also be considered for roles.

BATHGATE comedian Fern Brady admits she sometimes thinks she's common. Though she is quickly disabused of that notion when she watches the participants of reality show *Married At First Sight*, for that's when she realises with a jolt: "There's folk who don't know what coleslaw is."

DAVID Cowan, the Home Affairs Correspondent for BBC Scotland, has been forced to self-isolate after realising he was suffering from mild covid symptoms.

The prospect of being trapped indoors must be frustrating for an energetic TV reporter. Though this period of prolonged pause has been made more bearable after an old chum left a box of beer at David's front door.

"Suddenly ten days of self-isolation doesn't seem so bad," admits the commendably stoic broadcaster, who is now hoping that some charitable citizen will leave fudge donuts on his doorstep, to soak up all that beer.

COMEDIAN Craig Hill is an eagle-eyed observer of Scotland's street-life shenanigans.

He describes a recent scene he encountered, thus . . .

"Only in the West Coast could a wummin' walk into a hotel lobby at quarter tae wan in the mornin' shoutin': 'Anywan wantin' extra pizza? I've over-ordered.'

"This other wummin said: 'You're like a psychic, hen. I wiz just sayin', I could fair go a pizza right noo.'"

(And they all lived happily ever after . . .)

COMEDIAN Andy Cameron's first car was a Mini. One day it decided to grind to a huffy halt on the road to East Kilbride from Rutherglen.

Andy vacated the motor and attempted to discover what was ailing it by glaring hard at the engine and scratching his head.

At that moment a shiny Jaguar came zipping along the road. Andy waved down the driver in the hope of obtaining assistance. Out of the Jag oozed a stunning young lady, to whom our hero garbled some words, and somehow managed to ask for help.

She smiled sweetly, then purred in honeyed tones: "I'm awfully sorry. I can't help you. I'm a chiropodist."

Doing his best Cary Grant impersonation, Andy responded with simpering suavity: "Surely you could give me a wee toe?"

WHEN woke mobs started ripping statues from their plinths, the Diary wondered what could replace them, and truly there was only one possible answer.

New statues . . . of Lorraine Kelly.

Better yet, Lorraine's wise and noble features could be carved into the side of Ben Nevis, much as the faces of several American presidents are immortalised on Mount Rushmore.

She truly is the pinnacle of human perfection. Yet Boris Johnson doesn't agree, for when asked about the Scottish broadcaster during a TV interview, he scandalously muttered: "Who's Lorraine?"

Over on GB News one admittedly excitable presenter is suitably outraged, with anchorman Dan Wootton saying: "Everyone knows Lorraine. She's like Madonna."

At which point the Diary gets itself into its own spot of bother by muttering: "Who's Madonna?"

SCOTTISH broadcaster Paul Coia's daughter is disappointed a gig she was attending was cancelled.

Paul wondered why it was called off. His daughter explained that one of the musicians has covid.

And the name of the band?

The Vaccines.

NEW ZEALAND based Scottish crime writer Liam McIlvanney is feeling anxious. And rightly so, with the disruption to global supply chains having far-reaching effects.

Liam reveals that it's now more than two months since a can of Guinness graced the shelves of his local shops.

"Surely some kind of humanitarian intervention is imminent?" wails the traumatised author.

DISTINGUISHED historian and prolific scribbler Niall Ferguson gives short shrift to lengthy treatises. The former Glasgow Academy pupil now plies his trade in the States, where he is a Senior Fellow at the Hoover Institute, and regularly advises prominent American politicians. He has also found time to complete nine major works of history.

But is composing weighty tomes worth the bother? Perhaps not.

Niall admits he writes books that are "far too long for anyone to read cover-to-cover".

He adds: "A book is now essentially a decoration in an office or in a home."

So how should a historian communicate his ideas to the great unwashed? "Ultimately you get to the point where you can express your most sophisticated ideas in a tweet," says Niall, adding: "Once we've done the unintelligible, we produce the tweet."

THOSE thrill-a-minute thespians Alan Cumming and Miriam Margolyes have been touring Scotland in a camper van for Channel 4 series *Miriam and Alan: Lost in Scotland*.

Alan was delighted the pair didn't have to sleep in the van: "That meant that all the habits that could have been annoying, like Miriam eating raw onions and farting loudly, were cute instead."

Miriam, meanwhile, revealed the downside of having a toilet-seat cover made in her own tartan: "I'm not somebody who likes fabric in a lavatory," she explained. "I think fabric should be in the gusset of your knickers and nothing else."

CONGRATULATIONS to pun-loving Fife comedian Richard Pulsford, who joked his way through to the finals of the Scottish Comedian of the Year. It's thoughts such as the following that have made Richard a triumphantly silly success . . .

"A French mime artist taught me that 'less is more'. Morsel, more so."

ROMANTICALLY inclined Glasgow actor Johnny Mac has been mulling over the meaning of amour, eventually arriving at the following description . . .

"The definition of true love: opening a chilled glass bottle of Irn-Bru and letting my wife have the first swig."

ROCK musician Paul Simpson is a Scouser who has recently moved to Glasgow, and he finds himself more than a tad perturbed by the culinary delights on offer in his adopted hometown.

For the very first time he has been confronted by that darkened, doughy delicacy that is the well-fired roll.

Paul – who has played with several bands, including The Teardrop Explodes – notes that the rolls are promoted as being baked at a higher temperature.

"Higher temperature than what?" he wonders. "The surface of the sun?"

After studying the list of goodies that go into making each roll, he adds: "That's a long list of ingredients . . . for carbon."

ENGLISH rap music star Zuby has also been informed about Scottish well-fired rolls, and he isn't happy about the situation. Dismissing our proud nation's greatest baking innovation, he says: "They rebranded burnt toast . . ."

AMERICAN comedian Jay Leno was paid oodles of dosh every year when he hosted the popular *Tonight Show* in the States.

Though he admits he always found it hard to impress his Scottish mother with Hollywood gossip.

When he first moved to Beverly Hills, Jay informed mum that Sylvester Stallone had recently been paid ten million dollars for two weeks' work on a movie.

There was a long pause, then Mum said: "But what's he going to do with the other fifty weeks? What if no other job comes in?"

FRAN Healy, the frontman of Glasgow band Travis, had his finger badly gnawed by a dastardly dachshund.

Thankfully Fran has now been through surgery and is on the mend. Or, as one fan described it to him: "So you're now Fran Healing?"

ACTOR Douglas Henshall's toddler celebrated reaching the grand old age of five with a party. Which resulted in Douglas's house being overrun by miniature revellers.

"They have revolutionised every room," shudders Douglas. "Sometimes you just have to stand back, applaud the sheer inventiveness of the carnage."

RAISE the Roof is the new album from former Led Zeppelin wild man Robert Plant and his country crooner chum Alison Krauss.

Intriguingly, the record includes a cover version of "It Don't Bother Me", written by the late Scottish folk legend Bert Jansch.

The Diary's favourite Jansch yarn involves him learning to play guitar in the 1960s.

Fellow folky Archie Fisher said it took him two lessons to teach Bert everything he knew about the guitar, even though Bert had never previously picked up the instrument.

Archie admitted it would have taken only one lesson, but for the first class the two men sneaked off to get stocious.

WE hear that actress Jane McCarry – who played Isa in popular Scottish sitcom *Still Game* – didn't cover herself in glory while watching an episode of TV quiz *Mastermind*. Apparently she only got two questions right in one of the Specialist Subject rounds.

Which doesn't sound too embarrassing. Until you discover that the Specialist Subject happened to be *Still Game*.

THERE'S oodles of dosh available when you become a big-time broadcaster. Just ask Radio Clyde DJ Callum Gallacher, who is in an ecstatic mood.

"What's greater than pulling on a jacket you haven't worn in ages and finding £1 in the pocket?" says Callum, before giving the only possible answer: "Pulling on a jacket you haven't worn in ages and finding £2 in the pocket."

THE vaccine rollout is running fairly smoothly, though we discover there has been the occasional "bumpy" moment.

Edinburgh radio broadcaster Lynsey Gibson was getting

her booster and had to take an arm out of her jumper, which wouldn't roll up.

After the injection was administered she started stuffing her arm back into the jumper. Which was when she realised her bra strap had fallen down, meaning a whole lot of Lynsey was on the loose.

"Fined for indecent exposure at the vaccination centre is the tamest thing on my record, to be fair," chuckles the red-faced radio rascal.

GLASGOW comedian Leo Kearse was on a TV show with fellow humourist Simon Evans. Simon bemoaned the fact that he couldn't enjoy a snack in a tavern he visited as the kitchen was closed.
With a sigh, he added that not even a Scotch egg was for sale.

"Sort of relieved you couldn't have a Scotch egg," replied Leo, "because that's where the next generation of Scotsmen will hatch from."

BROADCASTER Jeremy Vine received an auto-warning about his use of robust language on the social media site Twitter, after he wrote the word sh**e.

Twitter's reaction surprised Jeremy, who says it suggests "that no part of the company is Glasgow-based".

COMIC actor Greg McHugh famously plays the naïve and trusting Garry: Tank Commander on TV and in panto.

Though we learn that it is others who have been far too naïve and trusting when confronted by Greg's wily machinations.

"Growing up in Edinburgh, our landline number was one number away from the local Pizza Hut," he reveals. "We received calls daily for pizza orders. My dad always politely told them the correct number to call. His sons, however, regularly took orders with large discounts."

Regretting his youthful roguishness, Greg adds: "Apologies to those still waiting."

ACTING in movies is a glam biz. Fame, fortune and a professional coiffurist at your beck and call.

At least the Diary assumed this was the case . . . though perhaps not.

Glasgow actress Nicolette McKeown, who can be seen in the film 'Lost at Christmas' admits: "Styling hair is something I've always struggled with. I normally just let the wind style it for me."

SCOTTISH author David S Wills specialises in writing about those wild American beatniks who included amongst their number Allen Ginsberg and William Burroughs.

It seems that David's own behaviour is equally outrageous, for he reveals that he unknowingly poured the last of an expensive bottle of whisky into a mug full of ants.

"So now I'm drinking ants and whisky," he reports. "And you know what? It's not bad."

With mounting fervour, he adds: "Miraculously no hang-over. Maybe I should start adding ants to all my alcoholic beverages."

THE decadent writer Samuel Taylor Coleridge once woke from a bizarre dream that inspired him to write his exotic poem "Kubla Khan". Glasgow broadcaster Paul Coia is a more grounded fellow, though it seems that when he snoozes he becomes as cockamamie as Coleridge, for he recently dreamed that he was wearing full armour and was leading a medieval army on horseback.

"As we faced the opposing horde on the battlefield, their leader and I met in the middle," recalls Paul. "We decided there was no need for thousands to be maimed or killed, and we'd settle it by batting each other.

"The winner would be the one who was the best at . . . colouring in."

ENTREPRENEUR and regular on TV show *Dragons' Den* Deborah Meaden is spending three days in Edinburgh for her birthday. On social media she asks her followers what she should do in the Scottish capital.

Fellow broadcaster and west coast resident Muriel Gray helpfully suggests: "Come to Glasgow."

THE actor's life can be one of trial, tribulation and bitter disappointment. Jordan Young, the dynamic and youthful-looking thespian who is famed for his appearances in *River City* and *Scot Squad*, knows this only too well.

The other day he had a wobbly moment of woe when he realised he had a hairy ear, a sure sign in a bloke that old age and decrepitude are imminent.

"Turned out it was just fluff off a jumper," he sighs with relief. "Playing age still 20–26 . . ."

(He's actually in his forties, but – shhhh! – don't tell anyone.)

J.K. Rowling is a rather famous Edinburgh-based author you may have heard of. Though it seems her own family sometimes need a crash-course in facts about Mum.

"One of my children was at a loose end one afternoon and went on one of those Potter walking tours with their best mate for a laugh," reveals Rowling, who adds: "They came home with a ton of information that was news to me."

EDINBURGH comedian and writer Martin Bearne is in an aggrieved mood. "So sick of them online scams asking for money," he huffs, before adding. "If you want them to stop, simply send me £9.99."

SCOTT SQUAD actor Stuart McPherson has been mulling over his many dazzling achievements.

Not quite managing to suppress a note of pride, he says: "My gravestone will read 'He was born. He seemed to somehow spend £30 every two days in Tesco express. He died."'

BOB Dylan performed in Glasgow's Armadillo in October.

But there was a catch. Anyone wanting to watch the frazzle-haired froggy voice in action had to dump their mobile phone in a bag in the foyer prior to the concert.

Diary correspondent Stuart Powell sputtered: "That's incredibly unfair. How am I meant to phone an ambulance to deal with my mangled eardrums when Bob starts singing?"

SCOTTISH actress Rebecca Elise was munching chocolates and saw what she assumed was a chunk that had dropped on the carpet.

It wasn't.

Instead, it was the brownish stuff that is regularly produced from the nether regions of her fourteen-month-old son.

"Only realised when it was practically touching my lips and I was overwhelmed by the stench," she shudders.

IT'S not easy being a professional entertainer, for it transpires that everybody is a critic. And we're not just talking about snarky homo sapiens.

Edinburgh comedian Rachel Jackson was completing an online form with financial services company Santander. One of the boxes she had to fill in asked for her occupation.

Unsurprisingly, Rachel typed "comedian". This instantly brought up the message: "Please enter a valid occupation."

A grudgingly impressed Rachel says: "What a heckle from Santander."

THE Diary is thrilled that Ncuti Gatwa is taking over the lead role in *Doctor Who*. Though some fans of the show are complaining that Ncuti – a graduate of the Royal Conservatoire of Scotland and former Dundee Rep performer – is a tad young to be playing an ancient Time Lord.

On social media one ardent fan of the sci-fi show has the perfect comeback.

Referencing the first chap to play the Doctor, Tom Pullin says: "Ncuti Gatwa is twenty-nine years old. The same age William Hartnell was when he was twenty-nine."

KERMIT the Frog celebrated his 67th birthday in 2022. Duglas T. Stewart, the frontman with Scottish indie band BMX Bandits, views the elderly puppet as a role model and one of his favourite singers.

"Terence Trent D'Arby once compared my singing to Kermit," reveals Duglas. "I took it as a great compliment."

POET and novelist Sally Evans runs a bookshop and bindery with her husband in Callander. Having a bindery on premises means there's usually spare leather lying around, which shop visitors try to scrounge for various reasons, including:

It's to leave out for the fairies in Balquhidder, in case they want to make a pair of shoes . . .

I'm a violin bowmaker, got any spare black bits?

I've burned a fag-hole in the pub upholstery and I dinnae want banned oot o there.

I'm trying tae fix the strap oan ma sporran . . .

BOOKER-PRIZE winning Glasgow author Douglas Stuart complained to a Norwegian chum about how something trivial had hurt his feelings. Being an empathetic soul, the chum turned to Douglas and said: "That makes sense. You're only hummus."

ROWDY rocker Liam Gallagher played Hampden. Reader Richard Davis was intrigued to peruse a list of banned and permitted items for the Glasgow gig.

Flares were on the banned list, which is understandable. Though our reader was more interested in the permitted list, which included, perhaps even more understandably ... ear plugs.

10

Cat Mangling for Music Lovers

THE name of the footwear worn when huffing and puffing in the local gym is trainers.

Or perhaps sandshoes.

Sometimes even sannies, for those who are too exhausted by their exertions on the running machine to wheeze out the entire nine letters of sandshoes.

In the States, the word used is sneakers. Which sounds rather sinister, like the sort of footwear an enemy agent would slip into in order to creep up on James Bond.

Whether you prefer the UK or American lingo, one thing is certain. Running shoes are highly prized objects.

In February, Sotheby's sold 200 classic pairs of the rubbery items for $25.3 million.

The Diary's financial department spent an afternoon figuring out what that amounts to in pounds sterling, before finally confirming it to be: "Pure loadsa dosh."

Clearly everything has a price. Which has us wondering how much Sotheby's would raise flogging Diary stories.

Of course, we'd never sell our treasures to the highest bidder. We prefer to give them away, at a bargain price, in the book you now hold in your hands.

Unfortunately even such a wondrous tome as this has its limitations, for regrettably the Diary Book can't be worn as footwear in your local gym.

Though as the following spirited tales prove, that doesn't mean this book doesn't have a whole lot of soul . . .

WITH a disappointed shrug, reader Yvonne Burke informs us: "I was forced to fire myself from cleaning my house. I didn't like my attitude and I got caught drinking on the job."

HIGHFLYING reader Henry Franklin gets in touch to explain: "You're not allowed to smile in passport photos because they want you to look the same as if you were standing in line at customs for hours."

RELIGIOUSLY minded Alastair Sillars from Dumfries recalls the minister of the kirk who informed his assistant that his bike had been stolen. The plan of action decided upon was that the minister would repeat the Ten Commandments in his Sunday sermon. When he got to "thou shalt not steal" the guilt-ridden thief would confess.

On Sunday the minister duly began his speech, but froze upon reaching "thou shalt not commit adultery".

His assistant later asked why he stopped.

The minister replied: "I suddenly remembered where I left the bike."

OBSERVANT reader Sharon Pilkington spotted a sign at the supermarket which read: "Chicken Strips, £2.50".

"I didn't even know poultry wore clothes," confesses Sharon.

FACEBOOK and other social media sites temporarily shut down for a few days, forcing millions of horrified users to engage with the real world for the first time in years.

Reader Derek Fletcher's wife mourned her tragic loss of precious screen time by piteously whimpering to her hubby:

"I've always wondered what a zombie apocalypse would be like. Guess this is the closest I'll get to finding out."

THE late uncle of Ian Noble from Carstairs village always took nine spoonfuls of sugar in his tea, though he wisely never stirred his cuppa, no doubt aiming to avoid any combustible chemical reaction.

Ian once asked: "Why NINE spoonfuls?"

"Because ten makes it too sweet," came the obvious reply.

ON a bus into Glasgow city centre from Shawlands, reader Sue Fletcher overheard a middle-aged chap say to a friend: "It's not so much that I mind my son fibbing all the time. I just wish the lies were a bit more believable."

With a world-weary shake of his head, he added: "I'm seriously considering enrolling him in a creative writing class."

IT'S been a while since reader Margot Walton had a holiday, and she admits to missing her jaunts to the snow-capped peaks that once thrilled her so much.

"My skying ability is going downhill fast," she says.

A NEW series of *Sex and the City* was finally broadcast. The original version of the TV show, about a gaggle of glam gal pals living it up in the Big Apple, was famous for its raunchy storylines, though the last season was shown way back in 2004.

"Even though the cast are much older, I'm sure it will be

just as racy," predicts reader Jane Barker. "Plus there will probably be some fantastic dialogue: 'Time to hit those nightclubs, girls! Just let me grab my Zimmer frame and hearing aid . . .'"

ANOTHER tale from the Big Apple, though this one isn't quite so torrid. Well-travelled Eric Taylor recalls showing photographs to his young grandson, James, of an occasion when he visited Brooklyn.

James was surprised to see in the background of one image a neighbourhood corner shop.

"I thought New York was too cool for corner shops," said the little chap.

"Well, New York has plenty of corners. Plus a few shops, too," explained Eric. "It would be a missed opportunity not to combine the two."

His grandson seemed satisfied with this answer.

THE editors of the *Oxford English Dictionary* have revealed the list of modern words that have been added to the increasingly weighty tome. Many of this year's choices are loanwords borrowed from the Korean language.

Reader Phil Edwards believes that dictionary compilers should instead introduce more examples of the Scottish lingo.

"You can't call it a proper dictionary if it doesn't include the word 'hingmy'," he argues.

FORWARD-THINKING reader Mandy Bourke says: "I find it helps to organise my chores into categories. So that's . . . 1) Things I won't do now. 2) Things I won't do later. 3) Things I'll never do."

THE above story reminds David Miller from Milngavie of a business-owning client who had on his desk an In Tray, an Out Tray and a Too Difficult to Deal With Tray.

THE previous yarn reminds Willie Ferguson of the time he was fixing the central heating in an empty office and spotted a small, round ceramic dish on someone's desk.

On it were printed in bold letters the cryptic inscription: round tuit.

The mystery of these words was solved when Willie read the line underneath: "Now that I've got a round tuit, I should be able to get everything done."

"IF at first you don't succeed," says reader Barry Walker, "skydiving is probably not for you."

READING the above Diary comment, Malcolm Boyd from Milngavie feels duty bound to add: "You don't actually need a parachute to skydive."

With a sage nod of his head, he explains: "You do, however, need a parachute should you wish to skydive twice."

OUR tales about the precariousness of sky diving reminds Stan Ireland from Kirn of a statement he heard about fungi: "All mushrooms are edible. Though some only once."

GLASGOW solicitor Matthew Berlow has made an unsettling discovery which could help him with his casework going forward.

"I found out last night that for years I have been telling Arab clients, who speak no English, that I am an engineer in Arabic, rather than a lawyer," he says.

No doubt his Middle Eastern clients are delighted to have Matthew in their corner, believing that in any problematic legal dispute, their engineer/lawyer will be supremely capable of throwing a spanner in the works . . .

CHATTY Larry Cheyne was yakking with his neighbour. She told him she had just had a man from a delivery van offer her a couple of "spare" beds at a reasonable price.

Quick as a flash, she replied: "That's a tempting offer. Can I sleep on it?"

THE religious yarn earlier in this chapter reminds Cameron Merriweather from Larkhall of a minister (not his own) who used to stand at the church door and shake hands with the congregation as they left.

One Sunday morning a young lad shook hands, and as he did so, pressed a ten pound note into the minister's palm

"Oh dear," said the minister. "Why did you do that?"

"Well," said the boy. "My daddy says you're the poorest preacher we've had."

SIGNING off an email to his granddaughter with the word "Grandpa", reader David Donaldson's predictive text offered two possibilities:

"xxx" or "died".

"Does Google know something I don't?" shudders David.

OUR story about the latest edition of the Oxford Dictionary reminds Robin Mather from Musselburgh of a couple of former bosses of his, both hailing from Glasgow.

When a new Scottish Dictionary was published they discussed their criterion for deciding on its quality, with one asking the other: "Does it include embdy?"

A DOORMAN guarding a pub in Glasgow city centre was spotted by reader Sarah Harrington patiently explaining to a drunken chap why he wasn't being allowed into the venue.

A second doorman, clearly disappointed by his colleague's conciliatory approach to the bouncing trade, scornfully said to him: "See, for being a big muscly boy, you're a helluva softy."

SCANNING internet news sites, reader Maurice Bruce came across a headline next to a picture of William Shatner, which stated: "Star Trek Actor to be Launched into Space".

Maurice says: "I was intrigued by the use of the passive in the headline, which implies that Shatner has very little say in the matter."

IMPRESSED by the above story, Iain Walker says: "It was fitting that William Shatner was blasted into space this week. After all, he did invent it."

(After much astronomical rumination, the Diary concludes that this is not the case. It's true that Shatner is an elderly thespian, though we have evidence that he was born a short while after the Big Bang, not before it.)

SOME astute financial advice from reader Ronald Hodkinson, who says: "If you really need to get a loan, borrow cash from a pessimist. He'll never expect it back."

FAN of all things spooky, Patricia West, gets in touch to say: "Make sure to buy your Halloween sweets for handing out to trick-or-treaters early. That way you have time to buy more Halloween sweets, once you've gobbled up the first batch."

WHEN reader Alfred Potter was thirteen he started learning the violin, and diligently practised in the bedroom he shared with his older brother.

Alfred's bruv was a generous chap who never seemed to be annoyed that he was forced to listen to a mere novice getting to grips with a complex musical instrument. He once even offered the young maestro a heartfelt compliment about his playing.

"That was smashing," he enthused. "I've never heard such an accurate rendition of a cat being mangled by a lawnmower."

THE twelve-year-old son of reader Ted Hosking asked Dad what it's like to be a grownup. In a moment of inspiration, Ted explained the exhilarating process of reaching maturity . . .

"When you're young, life is one big Chinese buffet," said Ted. "Everything looks appetising. And such variety! Maybe try this. That looks yum, too.

"Then you get older, and life becomes a burger van. And you better like burger, cos burger is all you're going to get."

Alas, Ted's son had no idea what his old man was jabbering on about. Though he did ask Dad if they could order a Chinese takeaway.

For some unfathomable reason the little lad suddenly felt rather peckish . . .

AFTER much lockdown disruption, academic life is returning to normal, with our nation's scholars applying themselves to what they do best . . . messing about like great big dafties.

At St Andrews Uni the tradition of first year students dressing in wacky costumes and battling on St Salvator's Lower College lawn, using the trusty weapon of shaving foam, has now resumed.

Combatants are never fatally wounded, apparently. (Thought it's always a close shave.)

GLASGOW criminal lawyer Matthew Berlow has bumped into the occasional nefarious character during his career. Though a visit to a Highland town gave him a rare glimpse of saintliness in its purest form.

"Tain is an honest place," marvels Matthew. "I left my wallet on the roof of the car all day, and it was still there when I got back."

Even better news. The car was still there, too.

WHEN October arrived, reader Lucy Hunter told us: "I was so relieved. All the dust and cobwebs in my house instantaneously became Halloween decorations."

AN inspiring story of struggle, strive and triumph from reader Nicola McNeill. "As a young woman I lived from one paycheck to the next paycheck," she says. "But through hard work and perseverance I now live by direct deposit to direct deposit."

WORRYING evidence that reader Darren Barton is toppling over the precipice into muddled middle age.

"I went into a place selling takeaway food," reports Darren. At the counter he said to the lady at the till: "I'll have one of your ... um, what do you call them? You know. A thingummy."

After a few minutes of such confused mutterings the serving lady expertly guessed: "Do you mean a kebab?"

He certainly did.

The name of the edible really should have been on the tip of Darren's tongue, as the takeaway he entered was named ... Kebab House.

FORMER Labour MP Sir Brian Donohoe gets in touch to give the Diary a proper scolding that we thoroughly deserve, after he caught us referring to Ayrshire's favourite bard as Rabbie.

Says Sir Brian: "Robert Burns was NEVER called Rabbie, as that was the name given to the village idiot, and if you addressed him as such he would have punched your headlights out."

The Diary humbly accepts the above clarification. Except for the part about Burns punching our headlights out.

The poet lived in eighteenth century Scotland. So he would have punched our candle lights out instead.

11

Space Walruses in Disguise

EARLIER this year the Diary was involved in a failed bid to purchase Twitter. (Elon Musk promised forty-four billion dollars for the social media site. The Diary offered roughly forty-four billion dollars less than that.)

Stung by our lack of success, we've instigated a new plan. Instead of buying a powerhouse media brand, we'll sell one, instead . . . ourselves.

That's right, folks. We plan on enticing Elon with the elasticated bank balance into snaffling up every single one of the Diary's shares.

For a mere forty-four gazillion bucks (our asking price) Musk can grab hold of everything that makes us great, including . . .

- Our glamorous city-centre headquarters. Or, to be specific, the dilapidated garden shed where we're based. (Euphemistically labelled Diary Towers.) Overlooking wasteland, it sports panoramic views of a rusty barbed-wire fence, a smattering of nettles and a grazing sheep called Barbara.

- Our spiffy coffee machine, available to all Diary staff. (Though in reality only used by Barbara, who refuses to let anyone else touch the contraption. She's very grumpy of a morning, especially before her first espresso.)
- Best of all – our humorous tales. The following chapter includes some of our finest yarns, proving yet again why we're the tops, not Twitter . . .

THE following ode, titled "Cycle Lanes" by Gordon Wright, is a tragic tale involving a chap's rocky road to despair.

Cycle lanes! cycle lanes!
These very words just fry my brains.
Then double yellow lines appeared,
The very things that we all feared.
Now bollards have arrived by night,
Another bloody awful fright.
Like aliens from the planet Zok,
All the neighbours are in shock.
A trip I had on a bollard base,
Sent me flying on my face.
I jarred my back and sprained a wrist,
Someone asked if I was p****d.
No use complaining to the City Chambers,
They are quite oblivious to these dangers.
I'm sending a letter to UNESCO,
I can't get parked at our local Tesco!
Don't tell me to walk, I'm not a sluggard.
Though if I can't park, I'm truly b******d.

INFURIATED Malcolm Boyd from Milngavie confessed to a friend that he had been shouting at the television. His friend admitted doing likewise.

"Should we be worried about this?" pondered Malcolm.

"No," replied his friend, who explained that he had consulted his psychiatrist son, who informed him that he only needed to worry if the television shouted back.

TELLY tales, continued. The favourite programme of Ian Noble from Carstairs village is *Later . . . with Jools Holland*. He adores the entire concept . . . apart from a couple of minor irritants. "I wish it was broadcast earlier," he says, "and presented by someone else."

ZOOLOGICALLY minded reader Ashley Harper says: "It's commonly believed that, next to humankind, dolphins are the brightest creatures. But it was a penguin who wrote all those classics. In your face, dolphins."

ARE extra-terrestrials visiting our planet, asks a startled Martin Morrison from Lochinver, having heard that scientists are using satellite imaging to count walruses from space.

Now, it could be that it's the satellites that are in space, counting walruses back here on earth.

However, without researching the pesky details of the story, our reader concludes that it is in fact alien walruses, travelling from the far reaches of the galaxy, who are touching down on our planet.

Martin is astonished that such outlandish visitations have mostly gone unremarked upon.

There can be only one conclusion. The walruses are in disguise, no doubt wearing long trench-coats with the collars turned up to camouflage their true identities.

So keep your eyes peeled on Sauchiehall Street, faithful

reader. You may just spot a space walrus searching for trench-coat bargains in TK Maxx . . .

EAGLE-EYED reader Ken Watson spotted some graffiti on a wall in Paisley, which read: "Yer maw's an Anti-Vaxxer. That's why they call her Mrs Doubt-Pfizer."

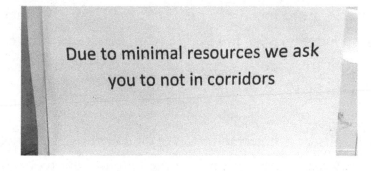

Due to minimal resources we ask
you to not in corridors

PRINCE William is meant to be a blue blood, though it seems increasingly likely that the stuff pumping through his veins is green, as in the political party. The earnest chap recently vowed to "repair the planet".

Reader Billy Webb says William's intriguing choice of words reminds him of his local car mechanic.

"Maybe we could fix the earth by having a quick look under the bonnet to make sure the carburettor's not kaput," advises our ingenious correspondent.

RELAXING in a Glasgow city centre café, reader Patricia Watts overheard a lady sigh despondently, then say to her chum: "If only life had background music, like in the movies.

Then I could figure out whether I'm in a romantic comedy or a horror film."

THE teenage son of reader Anna Nevill is considering career options, which is why he earnestly asked her: "What work can I do where I don't have to work?"

"MY uncle announced on his 75th birthday that he was taking up jogging," says Ian Noble from Carstairs village. "He very quickly reached his target of three kilometres per day. That was in 2017. We've no idea where he is now."

DOING his best impersonation of one of those knowledge-able chaps who turn up on *Antiques Roadshow* to examine random pieces of junk, reader David Donaldson once came across some posh porcelain cups and plates, which were embossed with close-up images of Michelangelo's starkers statue of David.

Our correspondent was very impressed, concluding that the plate would have been ideal for serving meat and two veg.

BROWSING in a shop selling musical instruments, reader Neil Ross spotted a middle-aged bloke buying an electric guitar. The chap explained to the salesman that it was for his teenage son's birthday.

With a chuckle, the salesman said that hopefully the lucky youth would one day become a famous rock star, then he could buy a private jet as a present for Dad, to show his eternal gratitude.

Dad answered: "I'll be demanding TWO private jets. After all, I'm also buying the lad a plectrum."

A TRAGIC tale of a career that careered into a brick wall. Stevie Campbell from Hamilton says: " I quit my last job, which involved me wearing a grey suit and cap while I drove businessmen around."

Our reader adds: "I put in a lot of effort, but at the end of the day the wages were so low that I didn't have much to chauffeur it."

TIME for some less-than-animated animal antics. Reader Tom Woodhead says: "If a sloth clapped, it would always sound sarcastic."

A TALE in this chapter about a lazy youth reminds Julie Harrison from Motherwell of the occasion her teenage son informed her that he had got his results for a series of school tests, and had only managed to score 15%, 10% and 33%.

Trying to make the best of a bad situation, the lad said to Mum: "If you add them all together, it's a pass."

"I'M so old," says reader John Chambers, "that I can actually remember getting through a whole day without taking a photograph of anything."

LESS-THAN-ANIMATED animal antics, continued. Reader Gordon Craig informs us of research showing that thirty percent of owners let their pets sleep in their bed.

"I tried it," says Gordon. "But my goldfish didn't look too great in the morning."

BUSINESSMAN Iain McDermid owns a licensed convenience store where an elderly lady recently brought a large selection of goods to the checkout.

The items were scanned and the total amount of cash due was requested by the assistant manning the till.

This turn of events greatly perturbed the customer, who said: "But all these items are from the free section."

Returning to the aisle which held the items, the old lady triumphantly pointed to a sign, then said: "See? It says alcohol free."

ON social media some arty types have been discussing the late, great Glasgow poet, musician and eccentric, Ivor Cutler. Theatre director Neil Murray recalls a Glasgow Green gig that Cutler performed in the 1990s.

It was a scorching July day, yet Ivor had a three-bar electric fire switched on backstage.

"And he stopped the show to berate a woman who took a Polaroid flash shot," recalls Neil. "He apologised, then said, 'But it was very rude!'"

A WORRYING thought from reader Tony Caldwell, who says: "Most working professionals would understandably get in a great deal of trouble if they hugged their clients without permission, or decided to kill them. Yet for some reason vets get away with it all the time."

A *HERALD* article reported that Knox Academy in East Lothian is reducing the number of times the school bell rings to create a quieter, calmer atmosphere.

An intrigued Iain Mills from Largs wonders if the real reason the action was taken was because the headteacher is eager to win a No Bell, Peace Prize.

ANOTHER tale about those teenage geniuses who in a few short years will take charge of our world.

Heather Lees tells us her daughter returned from school and informed mum that she had failed tests in History, Maths and English. Rather surprisingly, the youngster proceeded to say it had been "the best day ever".

Mum wondered how this could be.

"I had a Big Mac for lunch," sighed the contented youth.

THERE are some wonderful bargains on offer. For instance, Paul H. Costello tells us that he sent emails to over 300 customers while promoting the holiday homes and lodges that he sells.

Unfortunately autocorrect changed the wording in the message. So instead of including free Wi-Fi, the promotion promised a free wife with every purchase.

Having offered free internet deals in the past, Paul was intrigued by the response to his latest offer.

"Free wife got less interest than free Wi-Fi," he reveals.

WE continue with our tales of teenagers and their strange ways. The son of reader Iris Leslie arrived back from watching a football match and enquired if there was anything to eat in the house.

His mother confirmed that there was.

In a grumpy tone, the youth then said: "Do you mean actual food. Or are we talking about fruit?"

ON a bus into Glasgow city centre, reader Tom Philips overheard a young fellow say to his pal: "There's nothing you can do about it. You're going to have to take the bull by the horns."

The other chap wasn't greatly impressed with this advice.

"I totally hate that phrase," he groaned, adding: "Why would anyone in their right mind go near a bull, especially its nippy bits? I'd rather sneak up on a cow's udders."

VISITING a coffee shop in Glasgow's West End, reader Julie Bartlett overheard a lady at a nearby table say to her friend: "The nights are fair drawing in."

"You're not wrong," agreed her friend, who added: "These autumn evenings are like my ex's heart. Dark and cold."

OUR tale about a hungry but cautious teenager reminds David Donaldson of the years when his children were small, and soup was a handy stand-by meal. The conversation between the kids and David's wife Marion usually went like this:

Marion: Would you like some soup?

Kids: Did you make it?

Marion: No.

Kids: Yes, please.

12

Diabolical Sadists and Deep-Fried Snails

THE latest cinematic offering starring the surly bloke in the bat suit hit movie screens in March. Rather imaginatively it was titled . . . The Batman. Which is a refreshing departure from the first such blockbuster, released in 1989, which was titled Batman. (Minus a 'The'.)

The new flick was partially filmed in Scotland, with Glesga standing in for Gotham. Which is an ungainly fit. For Gotham is a crime-ridden, corrupt, filthy hellhole, while Glasgow . . . also has a bendy bridge.

It's strange to see a big-screen superhero romping round the Dear Green Place.

Though perhaps not that unusual, for as the following tales underline, Scotland has many dynamic dudes and dames.

Or do we mean deeply dippy dafties?

SPORTS fan Alf Munro used to work as a boxing club trainer in Glasgow's East End. To get youngsters interested in the pugilistic art he visited a local school to give a talk.

After he explained what professional fisticuffs was all about, he let the youngsters study the gym equipment he brought along, including a pair of boxing gloves.

One inquisitive scholar thrust a hand in the air.

"Yes?" said Alf.

"They shouldnae be called boxing gloves," said the earnest youth. "Urnie they just squidgy mittens?"

PICTURE fan Gordon Wright runs a photo library. On one occasion a book editor from London wrote to say he was coming to Edinburgh and would like to call in to see if Gordon had a selection of images of a particular Scottish writer. Gordon wrote back saying the chap would be "welcome to rummage through my files".

Regrettably there was no reply to this friendly missive.

Several months later Gordon was sorting out a pile of copy letters and came across the message to the London correspondent, and realised why the conversation had been so dramatically curtailed.

What Gordon had actually typed was: "You are welcome to rummage through my flies."

"I USED to own a swear jar," says reader Barry Stewart. "But I changed it to a pessimism jar. Now every time I get negative feelings, I put a coin in. It's currently half empty."

TUGGING on a pair of stout walking boots, the Diary braces itself for a precipitous hike, as we clamber upwards into the clouds, accompanied by Ian Noble from Carstairs village, who is determined to take us on a trek into the moral high ground.

"I'm appalled that many people seem totally unable to make a point on social media without descending into using profanity," harrumphs Ian. "What the **** do they teach at school, these days?"

ENTREPRENEURIAL Susan Crawford has ambitions to open a restaurant named Karma. "There will be no menu," says Susan. "You'll get what you deserve."

THE granddaughters of Bob Jamieson have been reading *The Lord of the Rings*, which has inspired them to dress as Hobbits on Halloween.

They also suggested that Bob join them, dressed as a wizard. "You could be Grandalf," they said.

A FRIEND of reader Tony Miller got a job as a chiropodist. The first day was difficult. "I guess he was still finding his feet," says Tony.

MORE job jabber. Roddy Young recalls the occasion when his local hostelry offered a teenage recruit a trial shift from 5pm to 7pm.

Unfortunately 5 o'clock came and went, with no sign of the wannabe bartender. In the same manner, 6 o'clock passed.

All was made clear when the young chap eventually strolled through the door for his shift . . . at 6.55pm.

ANOTHER tale of teenage travails. Donna Lawrence was on a train travelling to Glasgow with her son, who was looking forward to celebrating his sixteenth birthday with lunch and a visit to the cinema.

A conductor arrived and asked for tickets, and Donna proudly informed the chap that her son had just reached adulthood.

"Welcome tae the real world," said the rather grumpy-faced conductor. "Yer nae gonnie like it."

THE Diary isn't merely a literary masterpiece, to be discussed in the same hushed and reverential tones as the works of Shakespeare, Burns and that chap who devises all those pithy comments stuffed inside Fortune Cookies.

We are also respected in scientific circles, especially when it comes to our painstaking fieldwork.

For example, Diary correspondent Roderick Archibald Young gets in touch to say: "Research shows that six out of seven dwarves aren't Happy."

IT has been reported that 322 electric vehicles were left to gather dust in Glasgow car parks for almost two years as covid restrictions prevented council staff from being trained to use them. A Diary reader is not impressed.

"They weren't able to learn how to drive electric cars?" he scoffs. "What sort of deprived childhoods must these council workers have had that they never went to a funfair and got behind the wheel of a dodgem?"

STROLLING round the aisles of her local supermarket, reader Glynis Porter spotted pills for back pain . . . on a bottom shelf.

"Clearly shelf stockers are diabolical sadists," concludes Glynis.

EAGLE-EYED reader Eric MacDonald spotted an article in *The Herald* which reported that the leader of the Howard

League in England, who promote penal reform, is the rather intriguingly named . . . Frances Crook.

INQUISITIVE reader Mike Harvey says: "If McDonald's sold deep-fried snails in their restaurants, could you really call it fast food?"

WE continue mulling over molluscs in motion. Alan Walker from Carradale recalls the shellshocked snail who limped into a police station.

"I was beaten up by this horrible tortoise," sobbed the poor little fellow to the desk sergeant.

"If we find the miscreant, will you be able to recognise him?" enquired the cop.

"I doubt it," sighed the snail. "It all happened so quickly."

ANOTHER story of a genius teen. Mary Shelton's fourteen-year-old daughter told Mum she's thinking about studying acting as she has a great deal of talent in that department. Mum asked what gave her that idea.

"Well," said the youngster, "whenever you give me a birthday card with money in it, I'm brilliant at pretending I don't notice the money, and that I'm actually interested in reading what you wrote in the card."

SARTORIALLY minded reader Rob Truster shocks the Diary with the following revelation: "If you're not wearing any outerwear then your underwear isn't under anything, so you're not wearing any underwear either."

A CHAP was walking his dog in East Lothian and got chatting to a lady who was also perambulating with a pooch.

This lady explained that she's known as Vivaldi. Asked if she came by this moniker because of an aptitude for music, she explained that, regrettably, this was not the case.

It transpired that her given name is Viv, and she works for a popular German discount supermarket.

THIS autumn, as always, clocks were wound back an hour. Yet the husband of reader Carol Murray admitted finding it difficult getting his head round the change.

To ensure that he's fully acclimatised, he proposed that for the few days leading up to the climactic clock-winding event he should saunter over to the pub for his daily 7 o'clock tipple at 6pm instead.

Carol complimented hubby on his forward (backward?) thinking, then suggested an alternative idea. On the relevant days he should wake an hour early and do household chores.

"And," she added, definitively, "no clocking off."

A SPOOKY tale. "After spending Halloween running round dressed as a zombie," says reader David Young, "I'll be dead on my feet."

SOCIAL media site Facebook has rebranding itself as Meta. This rather meaningless and malleable moniker suggests to Diary correspondent David Donaldson that the company is eager to widen its field of operations and may soon launch the following services . . .

Meta Betta – online gambling

Meta Feta – cheese sales

Meta Detta – payday loans

Meta Veta – pets health insurance

Meta Wetta – incontinence products

WE'RE always glad when Halloween is over for another year. Not because the Diary team is terrified of ghosties and ghoulies. It's just that we grudge having to hand over our stash of sweeties to strangely attired children who impertinently knock on our drawbridge here at Diary Towers.

Talk of the haunting season reminds us of a comment from reader Andrew Robinson, who said: "I've just figured out that ghosts are people who died trying to fold a white fitted sheet."

TWO intriguing *Herald* articles caught the attention of reader Doug Maughan. One story reported that there are over a million rats in Glasgow. The other noted there are a quarter of a million homeless cats in UK towns and cities.

"If we could find a way of bringing these two problems together, we'd have a solution," says Doug. "Anyone know a feline Pied Piper of Hamelin?"

THE Scottish weather is doing its Scottish weather thing again. The thing it's been doing for thousands of years. Yet it still manages to intrigue the natives.

Standing at a Motherwell bus stop, reader Pam Moore heard an elderly chap mutter to his wife: "Ach, it's that wet rain again. I can put up wi' a lot. But no' the wet rain."

A FOODY thought from reader Tony Bleeker, who says: "Every knife is a butter knife. Butter ain't so tough."

WE mentioned that Facebook has changed its name to Meta. Reader Raymond Hutton informed his son, who asked: "What's a meta?"

"Nothing," replied Raymond. "What's a meta with you?"

13
Good Sports

IN January 2022 actor and chat-show host James Corden revealed that he'd shed two stone on a Weight Watchers programme.

This news inspired the Diary's squad of portly reporters to discuss whether we should likewise cut down on the mountain of munchies we chomp in any given week.

Alas, we concluded that there's a fat chance of that happening. For it's only by wining and dining our numerous contacts that we manage to accumulate our many exclusive tales.

So the next time you spot a member of the Diary's hard-working editorial team looking red-faced and bleary-eyed in a swanky restaurant – as they gobble and slurp their way through caviar, truffles, lobster, roast swan and champagne – have the decency not to interrupt.

For that valiant journalist is unflinchingly working on your behalf.

Regrettably there are some people who don't have the Diary team's discipline for dissipation. These people are called athletes, and they should be pitied.

Here's some tales about that most unfortunate breed . . .

A SPORTING lesson from reader Keith Wright. "Heading a ball with accuracy and power proves that a player has a great deal of skill and dynamism," explains Keith. "Though it's still not advisable while bowling."

THE Diary has proof that Scottish footy fans are of a genteel vintage; as sophisticated and well-bred as any peer of the realm.

Reader Becky Burns was in a bus leaving Glasgow city centre, a few hours before Scotland played Israel at Hampden, when she glanced out the window at a passing taxi.

The back door of the cab swung open and a bloke bedecked in tartan regalia leaned out before vomiting prodigiously on the road.

He then swayed back into the cab, slamming the door shut.

Says Becky: "Clearly this chap understood that it's more polite to hurl one's partially digested breakfast out of the cab, rather than spraying it over the back seat. Such a nuanced approach to etiquette! Surely this is the very fellow to take home and introduce to Mama and Papa."

THE girlfriend of reader Frank Marshall agreed to watch the Scotland–Israel match with him, even though she had happily managed to avoid colliding with the game of football until that very moment.

She proudly showed how rapidly her knowledge of the game was growing by saying at one point: "That referee is giving out an awful lot of yellow tickets."

SCOTLAND'S glut of goals against the Faroe Islands (a one-goal glut, to be specific) has footy fan Ken McLean enthusing about the sparkling performance: "Glad to see that our football team has reclaimed its position as one of the most covid-safe international sides in the world," he marvels. "By refusing to score many goals they prevented spectators standing up and cheering wildly, thus reducing viral transmission significantly. Good on you, lads!"

THE International Handball Federation has responded to accusations of sexism by changing rules regarding women's uniforms, and will now allow bike shorts and tank tops to replace bikini bottoms and crop tops. Reader Gavin Robertson believes other sports should also provide appropriate attire.

"Football is mostly played during winter months in chilly conditions," he points out. "So instead of wearing shorts and T-shirts, competitors should wear sensible clothing. I propose stout leather brogues, full length corduroy trousers, cosy Fair Isle cardigans and duffel coats."

Gavin adds: "Such a sensible ensemble would ensure our

brave sporting chaps don't fall prey to a severe case of the winter sniffles."

TANGLE-TONGUED Colin Robertson from Bearsden is struggling to pronounce the name of Celtic manager Ange Postecoglou.

Our reader has now resorted to referring to him as "pot o' glue".

"A nickname which I hope will stick," says Colin.

"STEVEN Gerrard has fled to Birmingham," notes reader Tom Cook of the successful manager, who quit Rangers for Aston Villa.

"He's swapped the home of Billy Connolly for Jasper Carrott-land," adds Tom. "So clearly no fan of comedy. Which also explains why he dumped Scottish football."

WITH Gerrard departing Rangers to wallow in the delights of Birmingham's Spaghetti Junction, Diary reader John Mulholland says: "I've just figured out why referees award Rangers so many penalties."

Our correspondent – who we assume is not overly enthusiastic about the Ibrox chaps – arrived at his findings by the scientific process of rearranging the letters in Gerrard's name.

Leading him to conclude that when it comes to dubious decisions in the penalty box, referees invariably . . . "rate Gers diver".

WE recall the chap in the golf club after the first day of the Masters who looked at the leader board on the telly and declared: "Will Tiger never stop his bad behaviour? I see he's chasing after Couples now."

A SPORTING insight from reader Jim Hamilton, who says: "Golf is an inspirational game because no matter how badly you play, it's always possible to play worse."

ARGENTINIAN kickyball king Lionel Messi won the prestigious Ballon d'Or footballing award last December.

We're not entirely sure that Stirling novelist Ross Sayers is overly impressed by this magnificent achievement, when he says: "Is it just a coincidence that Ballon d'Or is an anagram of Dr Balloon?"

CURIOUS Stevie Campbell from Hamilton wonders if there's any truth to the rumour that a scandal is about to erupt concerning systemic bullying of football match officials.

"Apparently it's been brought to light by a whistleblower," says Stevie.

"I USED to think badminton was the least-fun game played with rackets," says reader Kevin Delaney. "Then I played a round of worseminton."

AN East Dunbartonshire resident tells us that on the Friday after Celtic disappointingly drew with St. Mirren, a chum of his spotted a fellow wearing a Hoops top lurking in Cadder cemetery, and remarked to his companion: "Surely he's no' here to bury Celtic's title hopes?"

THE Diary has been patiently waiting for Scotland to conclusively prove it's the mightiest sporting nation on the planet, ever since our footy team suffered that minor setback in 1978, when we didn't quite shake them up. (Or win the World Cup, as we threatened to do in our pre-tournament jingle.)

Now the fallow years are over. Peter Wright, that majestic athlete and mighty Mohican of a man, has triumphed for Scotia in the World Darts Championship.

Reader Phil Sanders was on the edge of his seat watching

the final on TV, though his wife, sitting next to him, wasn't nearly so impressed by the sporting spectacle.

"So this is what happens when you give Sumo wrestlers jaggy bits of metal," she shrugged.

THE Diary may swoon over the achievements of darts champ Peter Wright. Though for some unfathomable reason not all of our readers are persuaded of the sporting prowess of the arrow-chucking fraternity.

While watching darts on telly, Mark Davidson explained to his wife that the commentator was a former darts player.

This revelation astonished Mark's missus.

"How do you end up a retired darts player?" she enquired. "It's not as though you can become any less fit."

SPENDING long hours in pursuit of a small, dimpled ball has given golfers a keen understanding of the trials and tribulations that life can offer.

Reader Jim Morrison overheard two sporting chaps chatting at his local club. Said one golfer to the other: "I'm awfa mixed up these days, Dougie. Between bird flu and covid, ah don't know whether to chase a booster or dodge a rooster."

GOLFING tales, continued. Russell Smith from Largs informs us of an update to the lexicon used by players of the game.

Apparently when a golfer is confronted by a tricky wee five footer, it's referred to as a . . . Sturgeon.

WE continue examining the arcane lexicon used by golfers. A reader tells us that when the ball races along, close to the ground, it's known as a . . . Liz McColgan.

MURRAY Macmillan from Bridge of Allan explains that a "Glenn Miller" is when the ball doesn't make it over the water.

THE Diary recalls the days when the tactics of a footy game involved a bunch of chaps scampering around on a pitch, while some other bloke in a suit yelled at them from the bench to run faster, tackle harder, and try to break a few shinbones before the half-time orange.

Nowadays the game's more complex. You have people whose job titles sound incredibly grand, such as Marta Rams Aragay, who has been hired as First Team Performance Analyst at Aberdeen FC.

One thrilled fan has messaged Marta, saying: "Welcome rae Eberdeen quine, noo gaan n get yersel a puckle o butteries for yer brakfist."

We assume that before Marta focuses on team performance, she'll have to put in a serious shift analysing that message . . .

WATCHING the football semi-finals of the Spanish Super Cup, Ron Beaton from Dunblane was reminded of a memorable character portrayed by comedian Rikki Fulton in his classic *Scotch and Wry* television show. A member of the Glasgow constabulary who boldly sat astride a motorcycle, and whose goggles tended to ping off into the distance whenever he hoiked them from his helmet.

For there in the Spanish stadium, on a billboard emblazoned in huge letters, was the word . . . SUPERCOPA.

WE continue celebrating arcane golfing terminology. Bill Rutherford from Galashiels tells us that an unfortunate lie of the ball is sometimes called a "Piers Morgan".

This is when you really want to give it a good smack, but, regrettably, can't.

MORE golfing terminology. Alan Walker from Carradale informs us that some rather ungallant golfers have shamefully named a shot that is thinned and keeps going a "Sally Gunnell", for it's not especially attractive, though it is a good runner.

WATCHING the golf from Carnoustie, Jim Morrison noticed that one of the female players was on the score sheet as Y. Noh.

Our reader is eager to know if she has a pair of delightful sisters called How and Gonnie.

EARLIER this year, footy fan John Mulholland found himself concerned about our nation's nebulous chance of grabbing glory on the international stage: "If Scotland fail to qualify for the football World Cup finals in 2022, I will never again mention Qatar . . . it'll just stick in my throat."

RIVER CITY star Jordan Young is a diehard Rangers fan. Though being an actor, he recalls the experience of watching Rangers lose in the 2022 Europa League final as though it was the blurb for a movie poster.

"Twenty-four hours in Seville," says Jordan. "Lost on penalties, lost my phone, lost my voice. One man's touching struggle with loss."

WE hear of a Scotland footy fan who found himself visiting Scottsdale, Arizona. On asking for a liquid refreshment he was promptly handed an amber ale called Kilt Lifter.

"Must have known I was arriving," he concluded.

ENGLAND winning anything is invariably viewed as a provocation aimed at the Scottish nation; they only do it to spite us, after all.

Nevertheless, there is an upside to the Lionesses' footy

victory at Euro 2022. It inspires the argy-bargy bards of Alba to scribble poetry in retaliation, such as the following verse from Gavin Weir of Ochiltree . . .

> Ochone, ochone. Gawd, help me, Mither,
> England's went an' scored anither.
> "Haun ba', haun ba," the Germans shout,
> But England's won the cup, nae doubt.
> Ending the pain o' a long, winless drought.
>
> Sixty years o' hurt, now done an' gone,
> '66 and '22, on Wembley's fabled lawn.
> But if you're a Scot, and you live tae a hunner,
> The BEEB will showcase the win – a weekly repeat stunner,
> And for the next sixty years, our lives will be a scunner.

14

More from the Diary's Resident Guru . . .

ONCE again the Diary's esteemed Editor has been temporarily let loose upon a scrap of A4 paper, so that he can make his views known to the great unwashed.

Of course, what the great unwashed really need is a bar of soap and a loofah, not some daft witterings from our boss. But until a slab of Imperial Leather becomes available, this will have to do . . .

BEING the UK's most illustrious journalist is a marvellous occupation.

Showbiz buddies always invite me to glamorous parties in penthouse suites, where we swap bon mots and tittle-tattle every bit as naughty and sparkling as the champagne being quaffed. (Moët & Chandon, of course. None of your Tesco own brand rubbish.)

I also have the ear of every politician of good standing in Westminster and Holyrood. If there's a government policy worth admiring, it was my advice that led to its unveiling.

A policy universally condemned? I was holidaying at the time. The minister tried to get through on my mobile, to beg for advice. Alas, I was busy at the pool bar, explaining to a grateful Leonardo DiCaprio how to introduce emotional integrity into his next performance.

But sometimes even a premier wordsmith gets a little antsy, and yearns for a new challenge. That's why I've decided to start my own religion. Nothing fancy. All I intend to do is introduce a moral and social framework to be obeyed by all mankind, that also explains how the universe began, and what to expect from an afterlife.

First I need some catchy sloganeering. Pithy one-liners summing up my message to the faithful. And I can now proudly proclaim that I've found the source of some instant wisdom . . . by tearing off the lid of a Pot Noodle.

What I spotted inside was dried noodles, inevitably. Though they were less important than something else I discovered.

A sachet.

Of sauce.

Written on the sachet was a message. No, not just a message. A commandment, much like the words scrawled on those chunks of rubble discovered by some beardy bloke on Mount Sinai.

What was written was this: "Squeeze A Little Extra."

I sat down and pondered this for a long time. Isn't it true that we could all "squeeze a little extra" from life?

For many of us, the sachet of opportunity is left unopened. We are frozen to the spot, like dried noodles in a plastic pot, hoping the boiling kettle of inspiration will be drizzled over us, allowing us to flourish, to be flavoursome. To be delicious in our own special way. But no kettle arrives. And we have to admit that life has gone to Pot (of the noodle variety).

Having been inspired by the philosophical sachet, I decided to open another Pot Noodle, to discover if more wisdom lurked within.

I came across a different sachet, with a different message. "Unleash What's Inside" it advised me. Clearly the sachet was explaining that we should be proactive in our dealings. Don't wait for life to happen to you. You must happen to life.

As I was about to tear open a third Pot Noodle, my wife arrived in the kitchen.

"That's good food you're wasting," she snarled.

The Pot Noodles and sachets were ripped from my hands.

Perhaps I won't bother inventing a new faith just yet. Better to ensure my wife has a modicum of faith in me, first . . .

15

The Dangers of Unicorns, the Delights of Cheesy Wotsits

INFLATION became a serious concern in 2022, leading the Diary to charge our Economics Department with analysing what this meant for our own august organisation.

The financial wizards at our disposal proceeded to blow the dust from their wooden abacuses. They then whipped off their shoes and socks in order to evaluate complex numbers using both fingers and toes.

After hours of intricate calculations and heated debate amongst themselves, they presented the rest of the Diary team with a painstakingly drafted financial assessment for the year ahead, which we quote now in its entirety.

"Yikes!" is what they scribbled.

Clearly stringent cost-cutting measures had to be taken.

So we sacked the office butler and cut down on our daily intake of caviar.

But there's one thing we will never sell, no matter how precarious the financial situation. And that's our treasure-trove of tales.

They're just too darned valuable, as we're sure you'll agree after perusing the following gems . . .

CONVIVIAL Gordon Fisher from Stewarton was enjoying a meal with his family in one of East Ayrshire's finest restaurants. The Sunday roast was filling, so he informed everyone that he wasn't sure he could manage pudding.

When the waiter took the dessert order he changed his mind, and said: "I'll have affogato."

Gordon's eighty-one-year-old mother flashed him a look

which was both quizzical and disapproving. When the waiter left, she said: "No wonder you're getting a kite on you. You said you were full up and here you are having half a gâteau."

A METAPHYSICAL thought from reader Kenny Harrop, who says: "No matter how hard you push the envelope, it remains stationary."

THE mother of reader Mary Clarke enjoys knitting, often becoming deeply preoccupied in this endeavour.

"What's the big deal about knitting?" Mary once asked her.

"Well," replied her mum. "Before the invention of the mobile phone, knitting was the only way I could ignore your dad on a long train journey."

RELAXING in a Glasgow pub, reader Jeremy Worthy heard a chap arguing with his lady friend. The couple must have been preparing to go to a fancy-dress party as he wore an Elvis costume and she was garbed as a zombie.

In a hurt tone, the chap said: "You callin' me an eejit, likes?"

His feisty inamorata replied: "Put it like this. If I really were a zombie, I'd oany wanna eat your brains if I were oan a strict diet."

SUSPICIOUS Neil McIntyre from Ayr says: "Have you noticed that only one company makes the board game Monopoly?"

CREATIVE Bob McCall from Shawlands wonders if anybody will sponsor him to film a documentary set in an orthopaedic ward.

"The show will be called 'Dislocation, Dislocation, Dislocation,'" says Bob.

THE ageing process is truly delightful, like enjoying twelve rounds of fisticuffs with Tyson Fury.

With a resigned sigh, reader Rab Thomas tells us: "I used to hurt my back going over the handlebars of my Chopper bike, falling out of trees and playing rugby. Now my back hurts when I brush my teeth, cough or tie my shoelaces."

THE grimness of getting on in years, continued. Tom Graham from Troon recalls the two Ayrshire golf club members who were lamenting the problems they encountered as they grew increasingly grizzled, grey and gurning of face.

One summed it up thus: "This growing old is a b****r. I'm not going to do it again."

STROLLING in Muirend, reader Caroline Crowden spotted a young mother pushing a baby in a pram. The baby, who was clearly some sort of unruly troublemaker, casually tossed its blanket from the carriage.

In a cut-glass English accent the mother tried to reason with her child.

"Never discard what you care for, darling," she primly scolded, "and you know you cherish blanky."

The baby heeded these wise words not at all, and repeated the rebellious action.

Leaving the Diary to conclude that the world isn't going to hell in a handcart. It's a pram that will provide the locomotion.

CURIOUS reader Henry Thompson wonders what his parents did to forestall boredom before the Internet was invented.

"I asked my six brothers and three sisters," says Henry. "They didn't have a clue, either."

VISITING his local supermarket, Gary Forbes spotted Batman shampoo. Our disappointed correspondent says: "No idea why they don't also sell conditioner Gordon."

A FANTASTICAL thought from reader Martin Fenn, who says: "A truly wise chap never plays leapfrog with a unicorn."

OBSERVANT reader Doug Maughan spotted the van of a dog-walking service which was called "Ruff and Ramble", which our correspondent rather approved of.

"Even better," says Doug, "It was parked in Muthill, or Mutt-hill as I've heard it pronounced."

JUNGLE hijinks, West of Scotland style. Robin Gilmour from Milngavie recalls the apocryphal tale of the lion that escaped from the Glasgow enclosure.

Two wee boys rushed into the police station in Baillieston, shouting: "Sergeant, sergeant, come quick! It's the lion, the escaped lion. We seen it running down Errogie Street . . . the escaped lion, sergeant!"

The sergeant slowly lifted his head from the desk and said: "Listen lads, I'm here all on my own. So the lion will just have to fend for himself."

NOT everyone is as adept as Nigella Lawson in the kitchen. Reader Mary Broome says: "Rock bands who can't afford a smoke machine should hire me to cook at their concerts."

MOST people arrive at Glasgow's Central Station to catch a train, though there is the occasional person who prefers a spiritual journey.

At least we assume this is the case. How else to explain the appearance in the station of a huge statue named Beacon of Hope, which portrays a figure with its arms thrust ecstatically upwards.

Reader Dan Reid was feeling equally ecstatic when he spotted the exalted image, though not because of its optimistic message to mankind.

"I thought it was advertising a nearby savoury snack stall where I could buy a treat for my train journey home," says

Dan. "Imagine my disappointment when I re-read the sign and realised it wasn't called Bacon of Hope."

A TALE about the rough edge of romance. The lady love of Gordon Fisher from Stewarton once made a disparaging comment about Gordon's waist size.

Our reader countered by claiming that he merely looked as though he enjoyed eating sweets.

Gordon's other half dealt a knockout blow with the withering riposte: "Darling, it looks like you enjoy eating three-piece suites."

MORE on the impeccable culinary skills of Scots. Russell Smith from Largs has a friend who always knows when his tea is ready . . . the smoke alarm goes off.

OUR readers are always prepared for an emergency. Jim Scott recalls his first motor, a Mini, which suffered from an unstable battery located in the car's boot, though a gentle tap with a hammer always solved the problem.

One day Jim stalled at lights in Glasgow city centre. The chap behind, driving a Jaguar Mark X, tooted tetchily on his horn. So Jim grabbed his hammer, which he kept on the passenger seat, and bounded from his motor, eager to deal with his wonky battery.

What the chap in the Jaguar saw was a fellow racing towards him wielding the sort of hefty cudgel most often associated with a Norse god of thunder on the warpath.

No doubt assuming his window was about to be smashed in – and perhaps his skull with it – the poor fellow cowered under his dashboard while Jim proceeded to give his battery a teensy-weensy bop with the hammer.

SCOTLAND was experiencing the sort of woeful weather we all know so well, which lead Albert Hannah from Aberdeen to tell us: "It's been so windy that my wheelie bin is now on a speed awareness course."

CONVERSATIONS in Glasgow can be as surreal as a daffy Dali daub. Reader Maureen Beam was on a city centre bus when she heard one teenage girl remark to another: "Ma maw's obsessed with the royal family, though ma dad's no fussed. The oany hing gets him goin' is a pack o' Cheesy Wotsits."

A COCKAMAMIE comment from reader Ron Marshall, who says: "Shoes are just portable floors."

A GOLFING chum of Russell Smith from Largs asked a clothes shop assistant for a bunnet, explaining that he was a medium.

"Oh?" said the intrigued assistant. "Could you get in touch with ma auntie Janet? She died last week."

SURPRISED reader Rod MacCowan says: "Is there just the slightest irony that the hero dog who saved a British soldier in World War II, and was recently commemorated by the unveiling of a statue in Strathaven, was a German Shepherd?"

EAGLE-EYED reader Robin Gilmour from Milngavie spotted a notice on the back window of an SUV with a tow bar, which stated rather despondently: "If you can read this . . . I've lost a caravan somewhere."

OBSERVANT Malcolm Boyd from Milngavie spots a new BBC documentary about a hermit in the Highlands named Ken Smith. Our intrigued reader wonders if this happens to be the legendary scribe of the same name who once edited this yearly annual.

Alas, this would be impossible. For it is exceedingly difficult for a *Herald* Diarist, former or otherwise, to become a hermit.

To maintain the splendiferous palaces we reside in requires a serving staff of hundreds.

EDINBURGH based Moyrs Forrest informs us of a terrifying hazard to be faced by those braving the tram system in Leith Walk, where signs advise to: Beware of Pedestrians.

Undermining the hysteria, somewhat, Moyrs says: "Could it mean – Be aware of pedestrians?"

THE wife of reader John Mulholland is determined to add another room to their house by knocking down walls and building a fancy new kitchen.

"I can't agree with her, and I'm refusing to budge on the issue," grumps John. "If I glue myself to the kitchen floor in protest, would that be extension rebellion?"

THE ABOVE tale reminds Peter Mackay from Kincraig of a friend who wanted to knock two rooms into one.

"He now has a kitchen with a 24-foot high ceiling," says Peter.

16

Jet Set Chewing Gum and Blackpool Mermaids

BACK in May the Diary congratulated Dunfermline on being awarded city status, though without trying to diminish this momentous decision, we had to admit finding it strange that a city can just be announced into existence.

Surely there should be some sort of objective criteria for such a designation. A city should have its own cathedral, for starters. A smattering of skyscrapers would also go down a treat, plus at least one impressively convoluted motorway belching out tangy carbon monoxide for city-dwellers to savour.

But, no. If King Charles says it's a city, it's a city. Meaning perhaps one day he will confer city status on his favourite potted plant. Better yet he could give the honour to the Diary.

For as the following chapter proves, we're a bustling burg, and home to many energetic residents who are always up to something intriguing . . .

"ENTERING a teenager's room is a lot like a trip to Ikea," points out reader Eileen Murphy. "You pop in just to have a wee look, and end up leaving with six cups, two plates, four bowls, a tea towel and some cutlery."

WE'RE told the story of a former nurse who found herself a patient in hospital, and asked her visiting husband to "Bring the big box of chocolates in the kitchen cupboard". This was to be a thank-you present for the ward nurses.

Hubby knew the very box. The following day he brought it, carefully wrapped with ribbon, plus a card conveying thanks. It was duly presented, and gracefully received.

Some minutes later there were peals of laughter from the reception area.

The cause of merriment was the contents of the box. Fuse wire. Scissors. Bandages. Sticking plasters. And a 13-amp plug.

It transpired that hubby didn't know the very box. Just the very similar box . . .

OBSERVANT reader Michael Ross points out that: "Baby powder has a surprisingly low percentage of baby in it."

THE husband of reader Mary Kay was soundly defeated playing online chess against a computer. Looking on the bright side, he said to Mary: "Bet it can't beat me at the breast-stroke in swimming, though."

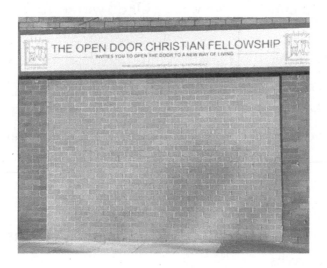

THE OPEN DOOR CHRISTIAN FELLOWSHIP
INVITES YOU TO OPEN THE DOOR TO A NEW WAY OF LIVING

SHAME-FACED confession time. Reader Fiona Coates admits: "I've done some terrible things for money."

With a shudder of disgust, she adds: "I'm talking about getting up when my alarm goes off in the morning, then going to work."

THE young grandson of reader Edward Deane came to him with a look of pity in his eyes, and said: "Grandpa, what did you do in your day, before the Xbox was invented?"

Grandad nodded sagely, and said. "We had our own version of the Xbox when I was a kid. It was called the swing park."

A TALE of true romance. Michael Watson from Rutherglen knew a nurse who tried to keep her relationship going with her boyfriend, who worked in South Africa, by chewing a piece of gum and posting it to him, so he could finish gnawing on it.

All together now: "Awww . . ." (Or do we mean: "Yeeeeech?")

WHILE studying at Dundee University, reader Paul Emerson played bass guitar in a local band at weekends. "We were called 'Wrapping Paper'," recalls Paul. "The reason being that we didn't have any original material but we could cover anything."

THE grandmother of Malcolm Boyd from Milngavie always used to say: "An apple a day keeps the doctor away."

Malcolm adds: "I don't know if that's true, or just one of Granny's myths."

"ARE your clothes too dirty for the closet, but too clean for the laundry?" enquires reader Olivia McBride. "That's what the backs of chairs were invented for . . ."

ANIMAL analysing reader Gavin Ferguson says: "Sniffing everything along a path while it goes on a walk is a dog's version of scrolling through its social media feed."

AMBITIOUS reader Mary Kennedy would like to grow her own food. "Unfortunately I've never been able to find any seeds for a steak dinner with champagne," she says.

A KILMARNOCK reader recalls a family visit to an aunt by marriage. Our correspondent believed this lady was talking about her mother in the present tense, so enquired how she was keeping.

"Whit?" retorted the aunt. "She's deid!"

Showing no attempt to spare the blushes of our poor reader, the aunt added indignantly: "And you were at the funeral!"

CURIOUS Stevie Campbell from Hamilton asks: "Is there any truth in the rumour that TV presenter Paddy McGuinness's younger brother Nick is in the first episode of BBC Irish police drama *Hope Street?*"

Adds Stevie: "I'm guessing he's the fellow playing a pub thief stealing pints from locals."

DOG owning Cameron Owen tells us that a neighbour brought his four-year-old son round to Cameron's house so the little fellow could pet a saveloy-shaped pooch owned by our reader.

The youngster was not impressed: "Daddy," he sniffled, "you said I was going to see a sausage dog!"

"But it is a sausage dog," his father patiently explained.

"It looks nothing like a sausage!" snarled the youngster, who demanded to be taken home.

The mystery was later explained when Cameron's neighbour phoned to say that the only sausage his son had been confronted by was the square variety, often found lurking in a Scottish breakfast.

"So you see," added the neighbour, "he was devastated to discover your dog wasn't shaped like a flattened-out brick."

VISITING a Glasgow hostelry, reader Ron Bentley overheard two chaps chatting at the bar. Said one to the other: "I hope my missus never forces me to go on holiday to Blackpool again. The trams on the promenade gie me the boke."

"Wit's wrang wi' trams?" enquired his drinking buddy.

"They're half train, half bus," shuddered the first chap. "Like a mermaid or somethin'. Nae natural."

VISITING the West Highland resort of Mallaig, reader Gordon Phillips and his wife went searching for lunch. Outside one local hostelry a sign read: "Warm welcome, and we have a coal fire in the bar."

It being a chilly day, such promises were enticing.

On entering the establishment, the couple saw no sign of a cheerfully crackling fire, though the publican helpfully gestured to a corner of the room, where there was indeed a fireplace, containing lumps of ice-cold coal.

He then smugly pointed out that his sign made no mention of the fire being lit.

THE doorbell of reader Mavis Coulter rang. When she answered the intercom a cheerful voice trilled: "Hi! It's the postie!"

Mavis was delighted.

"Professional people would be treated with much greater courtesy," she claims, "if they all introduced themselves in this chummy manner. Wouldn't it be charming to visit your accountanty, doctory and dentisty?"

THE wife of reader John Mulholland complains that he spends too much time corresponding with *The Herald*'s most popular column.

"I think she's Diary intolerant," sighs John.

ENTREPRENEURIAL reader John Alexander plans on designing environmentally sound office clothing using cactus leaves.

"My customers will be very sharp dressers," enthuses John.

IT'S reported that undereye circles have become fashionable with young girls, who use make-up to give themselves the appearance of bohemian dishevelment.

Reader Jenny Martin says: "I've craftily avoided having to buy such make-up by spending ten years on the night shift as a nurse."

THE Scottish education system is rightly celebrated as the world's finest. Like a conveyor belt of wisdom, it produces intelligent youngsters who boast a commendable knowledge of maths, science and particularly literature.

Proving this to be true, Ian Noble from Carstairs village

informs us that he overheard a couple of young fellows talking. The first chap told his chum that he had recently finished reading *1984*. "Tell you what," he added, "things were really bad back then."

THE linguistic prowess of our readers is legendary, though sometimes even they become baffled and dismayed by the complexities of the English language.

Luckily they often have a spouse who can rush to their aid, says John Mulholland, who provides us with this vignette of his family life . . .

John: I must be losing my mind.

Wife: Why's that, darling?

John: Well, I've been unable to think of a word play for strawberries, and I can't remember what the container they're sold in is called.

Wife: Punnet, darling.

John: I've told you already, I can't!

THOUGHTFUL reader Barry Hartnell says: "Paperclips are just staples with commitment issues."

SOME years ago, while visiting the Isle of Islay, Peter Mackay and his wife bought a souvenir T-shirt for a buxom lady friend. When she donned this garment, her husband rather indecorously suggested that it looked more like the Paps of Jura.

(Men! When will they learn to behave?)

THE young daughter of reader Coreen Barker revealed she never wants to go abroad on holiday.

"Why not?" asked Coreen.

"I only like British food," she explained. "You know, like Cantonese Chicken."

A PHILOSOPHICAL thought from reader Grant Anderson, who says: "Anybody who believes onions are the only vegetable that can make you cry has never dropped a sack of turnips on their toe."

OUR yarn about the chap who found George Orwell's novel *1984* rather confusing reminds Gordon Fisher from Stewarton of a girl he once taught who returned to class after an illness. She had missed a lot of coursework and a test on *Romeo and Juliet* was imminent.

With great confidence she assured her teacher that she would read the play that night in preparation.

Smelling a rat, Gordon warned her that watching the modernistic film of the same name, starring Leonardo DiCaprio, was no substitute for Shakespeare's original. The girl was outraged by such suspicions and left class with her Penguin Classic prominently tucked under her arm.

The big day arrived, and the girl's test paper started well, until she wrote: "My favourite bit was when he was being chased by helicopters."

17

Wall-Scaling Girlfriends and Galloping Poodles

ABBA are back performing live! Actually, what we meant to say is ABBA are back performing live . . . kinda.

That "kinda" is doing a lot of heavy lifting, we have to admit.

What actually happened in 2022 was that the Scandinavian super (trouper) group began playing nightly in London, in hologram form.

Some overly gullible fans claimed this was as memorable as watching the real Agnetha, Anni-Frid, Benny and Björn.

It's certainly true that animated avatars, created using advanced technology, can be useful.

For example, a hologram Boris Johnson would be far less likely to glug booze and chomp cake at illegal parties.

Meanwhile, Nicola Sturgeon could be presented with a life-size hologram of Scotland to play with, thus tamping down her nationalistic demands to a mild grumble.

She could even have her hologram nation apply for EU membership, then name it Sturgeondonia . . . oodles of fun to be had!

But a fake ABBA? Nah.

For such a hologram is unable to mimic the simmering tensions that famously exist between the genuine Nordic foursome. To be truly human, one must first be truly petty.

With that in mind, the following chapter sets out to celebrate our species in all its small-minded glory . . .

THE sweet smell of success. Reader Larry Cheyne believes that after developing popular perfumes for ladies, and after-shave for gents, Gucci should now target the youngest market possible by creating a scent called . . . Gucci-coo.

A DAFT thought from reader Oliver Wilkinson: "If you happen to find yourself completely naked but want to feel even more naked, put on a top hat."

A LEGAL friend of the Diary tells us of a relationship gone awry that reached the Inverness courts recently.

A bloke was indulging in some extracurricular activity of the amorous kind behind his girlfriend's back, though he assumed he was safe from discovery, being in the fifth floor bedroom of a hotel.

This proved not to be the case, for while he was otherwise engaged, his girlfriend bounded through the window, having clambered up scaffolding along the side of the building.

She was also brandishing a saw at the time, for what use we can only guess. Though on hearing this detail, the Diary's male staff members found themselves, for some unaccountable reason, squirming and crossing their legs.

Thankfully the jagged implement was never used.

The Diary's legal chum says the case resulted in him humming the song: "She Came In Through The Bathroom Window."

Though it wasn't The Beatles version that came to mind, but one by Joe . . . Cocker.

THE Diary finds itself recklessly leaping into the heated debate about whether you should put jam or cream on scones first.

"I always spread jam on first," reveals Ian Noble from Carstairs village. "Then I take a dollop of cream and rub it down the front of my shirt. That's where it ends up, anyway . . ."

FRUSTRATED reader Ken Bentham says: "I desperately want to buy one of those grocery checkout dividers, but the lady on the till keeps putting it back."

WITH the cold weather kicking in, Tom Wylie from Elderslie went to B&Q in search of draught excluders. Unable to find any, he asked a young employee sporting an "I am here to help you" badge where they might be.

Pointing to a far off aisle, he said: "Have you tried under doors?"

YEARS ago reader Barbara Smallwood studied at Glasgow School of Art. She never used her degree, and went into the restaurant business instead, though she still has an astute knowledge of what is deemed valuable in the art world. Which has led her friends to often seek her council regarding bric-a-brac they find in their attics.

She was once visiting a chum, whose husband showed her an old black and white picture of his policeman father in uniform.

"Do you think this is worth anything?" enquired this chap.

"I don't think so," said a rather bemused Barbara. "What made you think it had any value?"

"Well," said the chap, with the merest flicker of a smile. "It is an original constable."

SHOPPING in the John Lewis store in Glasgow, reader Jane Cameron spotted a little girl walking hand-in-hand with her mum. "We'll have to hop on the escalator, now," said the mum to her daughter.

"Which one?" asked the little girl. "The upscalator or the downscalator?"

THAT splendid musical *Les Misérables* was being staged at Glasgow's Theatre Royal.

Reader Mary Fielding was in the audience, seated next to a burly chap with a grizzly beard and numerous tattoos on his arms. He looked like the sort of fellow who would be happier straddling a Harley-Davidson than attending a night of show tunes. Mary concluded that the chap's wife or girlfriend must have dragged him along to the production.

"Then I noticed tears rolling down his cheeks during an emotional bit," says Mary. "I guess he really was a musical theatre fan. Or perhaps he was missing his Harley-Davidson."

A VIOLENT thought from reader Bob Pennington, who says: "Papercuts are a tree's final moment of revenge."

JOB advert of the day comes from a chap on social media, who states: "I'm working on something exciting and would love to hear from Scots actors, directors, musicians, designers, drag artists, fire-eaters . . ."

The Diary hates to jump to conclusions, though we're guessing this chap isn't launching a new accountancy firm.

A FINANCIAL query from reader Ken Davis, who says: "Why is it called bribery and not moneypulation?"

THE *Herald* reported the disturbing news that Heinz have launched Chocolate Orange flavoured mayonnaise. Smacking his lips with relish, culinary correspondent John Dunlop asks: "Can Irn-Bru flavoured brown sauce be far behind?"

OUR report about a burly Hells Angels type with a gentle disposition inspires Josephine Burns to tell us that she once dated a biker.

Upon visiting his flat she discovered that he was in possession of a small teddy bear, dressed in the same leather gear worn by his owner. The teddy was named Humphry.

"The soft toy was rather cute and showed the biker's emotional side," says Josephine, "though I dumped him soon after. It wasn't his emotional side I was interested in."

IT was reported that Noasis, an Oasis tribute band, got snowed in at a Yorkshire pub. Perhaps not the worst fate to ever befall a bunch of rockers.

David Will from Milngavie reckons the compulsory lock-in would have provided numerous opportunities for the imbibing of . . . Cigarettes & Alcohol.

(Wait. Hold on. Aren't ciggies banned in boozers? The poor rock and rollers must have had to survive on Alcohol & Alcohol.)

A PHOTOGRAPH of the Govan/Yorkhill ferry appeared in *The Herald*. A reader tells us he frequently travelled with his parents on the boat, and recalls its imposing notice, which read: "Drivers of horse-drawn and other vehicles shall, upon the vehicle coming to rest, scotch the wheels, both fore and aft, with the chocks provided for that purpose."

It was a different era, notes our reader. When horsepower meant exactly that.

TRANSPORT correspondent Garry Connolly gets in touch to say: "When you put a seatbelt on, you are wearing your car."

"GETTING fired from working at the Job Centre must be tough," says Scott Benton. "You still have to turn up at the office on Monday."

CLASSICAL music loving Colin Carpenter from Muirend was strolling with his earphones in, listening to Wagner's stirring "Ride of the Valkyries".

As the music reached its crescendo a chap walked past, accompanied by his pet poodle.

The dainty animal flounced along the path, though with the operatic music whooshing in our reader's ears, the dog took on a heroic aspect and seemed to be galloping like a mighty steed.

"Wagner is the mayonnaise of music," says Colin. "It makes everything juicier."

CONVIVIAL Douglas McLeod from Newlands attended a lunch with former colleagues, all in their late sixties.

They recalled a previous get together, when they were in the audience to watch another elderly colleague perform with his rock combo.

This fellow hadn't turned up to the latest reunion, and the chums scratched their heads, struggling to recall the name of his band.

The puzzle was solved the next day when one of the pals posted an email containing a publicity photo of the band, with their name emblazoned across the top.

How could the absent-minded oldies have forgotten that the group was called . . . Senior Moments.

A METAPHYSICAL thought from reader Paul Bury, who notes: "There is no precise measurement to indicate when a spoon becomes a shovel."

A TALE of a birdy with a biting beak. Reader Hugh Ferguson had a chum who was a fervent SNP supporter.

This chap owned a parrot named McTavish, who was trained to say "Who's a pretty boy?" when it heard someone speak in a Scottish accent.

When it heard an English accent it chanted something similar, though "pretty" was swapped for a word which, although rhyming with the original, had a very different meaning.

(In case you haven't guessed, we're talking about that unmentionable stuff that's often found lurking on the floor of a parrot's cage.)

OUR mention of the stirring operatic tune "Ride of the Valkyries" reminds a reader of the occasion he tried to persuade his wife that Wagner's *Ring* cycle was a new type of spin programme on the couple's fancy German washing machine.

WRITER Deedee Cuddihy recalls attending a funeral at Falkirk Crematorium. Following the service for a colleague she exited the building and was startled to see the chief mourner for the next funeral being helped from his car in handcuffs, a prison guard on either side of him.

"Only in Falkirk," sighed one of Deedee's fellow mourners.

A TALE of a schoolboy rebel without a cause. Gordon Fisher from Stewarton recalls a cheeky scamp he used to teach. This young fellow was leaving school one Friday afternoon, and Gordon said to him: "Have a nice weekend."

The grumpy youth snarled back: "You cannae tell me whit tae dae at the weekend!"

SOME advice from reader Ian Noble, who grouchily grumbles: "Young folk these days? They seem to get divorced at the drop of a hat. Why can't they stay together and suffer like the rest of us?"

18

A Delightful Name for a Wandering Emu

CHRISTMAS is coming, the goose is getting fat . . . or if the daft bird has any sense it's gone on a strict diet while putting in some punishing hours at the local gym. Those nasty humans are less likely to gobble it up if it's lean and ripped, rather than plump and juicy.

One of the Diary's favourite yuletide traditions is the ceremonial opening of the box of Roses chocolates.

Rapidly followed by the ceremonial complaint about the size of the box of Roses chocolates.

"In my day it was twice as large!" grumps Grandpa, who won't be placated until the rest of the family agree to let him eat every single one of those extra-yummy sweets with the purple wrappers.

Unlike a box of Roses, the Diary isn't shrinking. We're as big and buoyant as ever.

The following festive yarns, focusing on Christmas and New Year, are so good they should all arrive in purple wrappers . . .

LIKE a gurning Grinch, we've decided to list those hideously festive things we want banned this Christmas.

Karen Ralton says: "Yuletide drinks that crop up in Starbucks and Costa should be outlawed. Anything that's got a name like a 'Mocha-Frappu-Crimbo-Cino' or 'Turkey Giblets Latte With Whipped Cream and Blended Brussels Sprouts.'"

Our reader adds: "They taste disgusting and are incredibly fattening. Not to mention the price. Buy one and you'll be as broke as Bob Cratchit."

OUR Christmas banning list continues . . .

Jenny Fenn believes *The Snowman* cartoon, regularly broadcast on 25 December, should never be shown again.

"I don't understand why viewers are so emotional at the end of a film where a big pile of snow turns to slush," she shrugs. "What next? People getting teary-eyed defrosting the freezer?"

WE continue dispensing with Christmas traditions. Ross Doyle from Ayr suggests fun festive knitwear should go, especially as it often leads to marital disharmony.

"I was swithering about buying a humorous Christmas

jumper featuring Santa or Rudolph," says Ross. "My wife disabused me of the notion by saying, 'You don't need the help of a jumper to look like a moron.'"

THE rout of Christmas continues ... Cameron Smith suggests Santa should be fired, i.e. given the heave ho-ho. "He's overweight and elderly," notes Cameron, "which makes him one of those vulnerable folk who should practise social distancing instead of sneaking down strangers' chimneys."

BEING a bad guy can be very satisfying. You get to cackle maniacally whilst twirling your sinister moustache. You're also free to carelessly lob damsels in distress into crocodile-infested moats, or rope them to railway tracks.

Though there is a downside, as *River City* star Grant Stott discovered.

Grant, who is playing a diabolical scoundrel in *Sleeping Beauty* at the King's Theatre in Edinburgh, was confronted by a fervent fan turned fiendish foe.

He describes the altercation as the cutest heckle ever delivered in panto.

"Whilst in full evil flow, halfway through Act 1," says Grant, "a tiny voice bellowed at me: 'I used to like you!' Beautifully timed delivery, too."

FANCYING a night out, reader George Harper went to the Citizens Theatre production of *A Christmas Carol*. At one point children in the audience were encouraged to boo Scrooge, though George noticed an older chap also booing with gusto.

"Och, Tam," said this chap's wife. "Don't you be booing. Booing's for the weans."

Rather huffily, the fellow replied: "How come the weans get all the boos?"

"I'M invited to my neighbours' house for pre-Christmas drinks with nibbles," says reader Ted Murray. "They treat that flipping cat like royalty."

THE Christmas period is traditionally when the post office employs casual workers. Ross Cooper once spent a few weeks in December as a postie and was given helpful advice by a senior staff member, who memorably said: "If you're walking up a garden path and see a Rottweiler racing towards you, don't think twice. Run for your life."

"What if it's a wee poodle?" asked Ross.

"Not the same level of emergency," said the senior staff member. "So just stroll for your life."

'TIS the season to be jolly . . . or do we mean jolly old? Iain Mills from Largs says: "I didn't realise what an ageing population some Scottish coastal towns had until I found out their advent calendars came in blister packs with a pill behind each door."

IT'S the heart-warming innocence of children in an audience that makes pantomime such a treat. Gordon Fisher was enjoying the production of *Aladdin* at the SEC Armadillo. In the row in front was a small boy of about seven, with his grandparents.

It was clearly the youngster's first panto, and he didn't really grasp the concept of audience participation at first. But after some encouragement from Gran and Gramps he soon got the hang of it.

At one point the audience started booing the entrance of villainous Abanazar, played by actor Sanjeev Kohli. The wee boy was delighted to join in, and shouted with all his heart: "P**s off!"

As they shrank down in their seats, Gran and Gramps looked mortified.

A CRIMBO puzzler. Barry Nelson from Newton Mearns asks: "What's the most popular Christmas wine?"
The answer is, of course . . . "I don't like Brussels sprouts."

TWO buxom figures with garish make-up slathered across their faces were spotted just off Sauchiehall Street one late December evening.

Nothing unusual there, you may conclude. Sauchiehall Street at night is a noted location for ambitious young debutantes, anxious to claim their place in the upper echelons of polite society by getting pure stocious in the nearby watering holes.

But this was a different scenario. For the two figures were neither young nor female. (Nor were they particularly ravishing.)

It turned out to be burly Glasgow wrestler Grado, standing next to diminutive *River City* star, Stephen Purdon. The gruesome twosome were forced to flee their ugly-sisters routine in Cinderella at the nearby Pavilion due to a fire alarm.

"Belter of a Friday night," groaned a mortified Stephen afterwards.

PERSONABLE reader Gordon Casely wonders how he should forward his Christmas greetings to our daily newspaper column.

"Surely it is, 'Hark *The Herald* Diary'," he concludes.

"THIS year I plan on becoming a Christmas pudding," reveals Virginia Murray. "Small, round, drenched in alcohol and disliked by most people."

BRAVING the streets of Edinburgh to do some Christmas shopping, Mary Dawson found herself standing behind a chap in a toy shop queue.

As he placed an archery kit on the counter the salesgirl said to him: "If you want, you can have it gift-wrapped."
The chap immediately replied: "It's an archery kit. I assumed it already came with a bow."

"TODAY is my last day after thirty years' service working at the Christmas card decoration factory," sighs reader Matt Turner. "The end of a glittering career."

CHRISTMAS is often a time of strange occurrences and mystic moments, as any passing gang of three wise men will testify.

Faithful readers of this yearly book will recall last volume's Yuletide miracle, when we reported that large woollen tea cosies were appearing on top of Scottish post-boxes.

This year we've been provided with photographic evidence of a stray emu munching from a bin next to a bus stop in Livingston.

Locals have been debating whether it is Rod Hull's former

colleague, now fallen on hard times after the passing of the double act's senior partner.

Others speculate that it is an exotic Christmas treat, replacing the more traditional turkey, and now making a bid for freedom like Steve McQueen in *The Great Escape*.

The most likely scenario is provided by one witness who says with some authority that it is owned by a local cattery, and its name is Shirley. (Which the Diary thinks is a delightful name for a wandering emu.)

LAST year proved to be another difficult December, due to covid fears. Government restrictions hovered over would-be revellers, like a tinsel-wrapped sword of Damocles.

With a resigned shrug, reader Julie Daniels told us: "My Christmas tree lights went out more times than I did."

CHARLOTTE Mountford, the co-director of the Lyth Arts Centre in Caithness, is looking forward to Christmas, saying it's: "That time of year where we discuss what everyone calls a 'buffet style meal'. In my family it's 'picky tea'. But my fave is my brother's partner, who calls it 'stuff on a plate.'"

SOME people emphasise the cosiness of Christmas, as it brings families and communities together.

Not the Diary.

We prefer to focus on Crackpot Crimbo, a time of inexplicable happenings.

Reader Daisy Parker sends us a photograph she took this week of Glasgow's Duke of Wellington statue, famed for having a traffic cone on his head.

The cone is still there. What is new is that Santa has joined Wellington on his mount.

Some Scrooge-like souls may claim this isn't the genuine Santa, but merely an inebriated chap dressed as Mr Claus, who clambered onto the statue for a drunken dare.

The Diary scoffs at such an un-festive suggestion. Though we are concerned for Saint Nick. Riding a stone horse is bound to make Rudolph's red nose glow green with envy.

And who knows what a jealous reindeer is capable of?

THE teenage daughter of reader Tim Cole recently became a vegetarian. To show solidarity, it was decided that the family would enjoy (endure?) a nut roast on 25 December.

Yet when Tim went food shopping with his wife for the lunch, he was surprised when she plopped a turkey in the trolley.

"You know kids, always changing their minds," explained his other half. "My motto is: always have a back-up turkey in case of emergencies."

GLASGOW writer Ian Pattison is up and anxious on Christmas Eve, at 5.20am. "Poor sleeping pattern lately," he yawns. "Can't decide if it's existential angst or excitement coz Santa's coming. On balance, it's probably Santa."

MY worst Christmas present ever was a Bonnie Tyler sat nav," says reader Tom Davidson. "It kept telling me to turn around, and every now and then it fell apart."

BROADCASTER Paul Coia watched the Brooke Shields Netflix film *A Castle For Christmas*. "Supposedly set in Scotland, the accent coach misheard the brief," he says. "Instead of 'Jock' he's gone for 'Ewok.'"

THE Diary's crack troop of investigative reporters have spent the majority of this chapter unearthing those bizarre and brazenly bonkers stories that only seem to occur in the magical weeks revolving round Christmas and New Year.

We shone a light on the strange case of the wandering emu in Livingston. Then there was a sighting of Santa, merrily riding the statue of Wellington's horse in Glasgow.

Next up, a reader sends us photographic evidence of a chap who took an owl for a drink in a Paisley hostelry.

Or was it an owl who took a chap for a drink?

Probably not. Owls may be exceedingly wise, though they rarely carry a wallet about their person, which makes it almost impossible for them to pay for their round in the boozer.

CHRISTMAS is a time for the spoiled youth of our nation to wallow in all those expensive gifts they accumulated for no good reason. Glasgow radio presenter Amber Zoe points out that fun isn't necessarily something that has to be purchased from a toy shop.

"After all the money spent on children," she says, "I've just witnessed two boys having a burping competition sitting on the pavement."

CHRISTMAS is over for another year, though fond memories of family squabbles, indigestion and crackers going "pffft" instead of "BANG!" linger.

Comedian Andy Cameron's recollections go even further back, to celebrations of yore. Just after World War II he would help his granny pluck a festive hen, though only for Ne'erday dinner, for Christmas was a working day in Scotland. As time marched on the family graduated to eating chicken at Christmas, and steak pie became the Ne'erday treat.

"The chicken was always fought over by three uncles who demanded they got the drumsticks," says Andy.

With a twinkle in his eye, he adds: "My uncle Jim brought home an octopus one year so that everybody got a leg. This didn't really work as it kept reaching out of the pot during cooking and turning off the gas."

WHEN the wife of reader Colin Grayshaw caught him standing on the bathroom scales, sucking in his stomach, she chuckled and said: "After the Christmas dinner and Quality Street sweeties you've been putting away, that's not going to help."

"Sure it will," replied Colin. "It's the only way I can see the numbers."

A FRIEND of Ken McLean from Denny received a Lego-type model of the CalMac ferry MV Loch Seaforth for Christmas.

"I suspect it'll still be a work in progress for several Christmases to come," chuckles Ken.

CULINARY minded reader Kenny Hannah was disappointed when his wife offered him a turkey and Brussels sprout sandwich for lunch on 27 December.

"I thought we had the leftovers from Christmas dinner yesterday," he grumbled.

"We did," she replied. "This is the leftovers from the leftovers."

SOME gritty journalists become war correspondents in order to bear witness to man's inhumanity to man.

The Diary has an equally onerous task, for in this chapter we have reported on man's inhumanity to turkey . . . and sprouts . . . and pigs in blankets.

Kilmarnock novelist David F. Ross dares himself to deal with the problem of Christmas dinner leftovers. "Contemplating eating all the leftover cheese with no thought for the depravity of the dreams it'll prompt," he reveals.

With an insouciant courageousness to be admired, he adds: "This is the closest I'm ever likely to get to LSD. Bring on the dancing horses . . ."

RELAXING in a cafe, reader Beryl Hanson heard two teenage girls discussing Christmas presents they had received.

One disclosed that her parents had bought her a jacket, though she had decided to take it back to the shop and replace it with a longer garment.

She explained her reasoning thus: "I want something to cover my backside. In this weather I'd rather have a warm bum than a hot date."

ONE of the Christmas presents received by Matilda, the nine-year-old granddaughter of reader Bob Jamieson, was a game called Carcassonne.

Since receiving it she has unceremoniously dispatched anyone foolish enough to challenge her to play.

"Having been on the wrong end of a severe hammering," says Bob, "I asked her what the secret was."

With a mystical, faraway look in her eyes, the little girl replied: "Trust the Process."

SEEING the back of Christmas wasn't entirely depressing, for it meant that leftover festive food was sold at bargain prices in supermarkets.

Reader Gordon Nevill raced home to dazzle his wife with the tub of extra thick brandy cream he snaffled up in Sainsbury's, costing him a grand total of . . . one pence.

And was the missus impressed?

"That's the cheapest heart attack you'll ever buy," she shrugged.

THE revelries continue with purpose, as New Year beckons. Though politicians advise dialling down the delirium.

WITH Hogmanay almost upon us, reader Darren Burke recalls the occasion when he spent the festivities in Glasgow's George Square, and spotted a rather inebriated young woman, who at one point vomited copiously on the shoes she was wearing.

"Awe, look wit ye done, hen," commiserated an equally giddy pal swaying next to her.

"Nae worries," shrugged the vomiter. "They're your shoes, remember? I borrowed 'em off you at the start o' the night. Wan o' ma better ideas."

"NEXT year I'm going to dedicate most of my time to helping wildebeests suffering from hearing problems," says reader Pam Hannah. "It's my gnu ears resolution."

THE year 2022 crawled out of its weary bed, then staggered to the bathroom to gaze, appalled, at its bloodshot eyes in the mirror, while promising never to mix lager, champagne and steak pie again.

Many of our readers also regretted their Hogmanay celebrations.

Not Jack Branson, however. He admits that he preferred the festivities this year, especially as there was no outdoor partying due to lockdown.

"I usually go with pals to a Glasgow city centre bar to see in the bells," Jack told us. "Though this year, due to covid restrictions, I sipped a few cans alone in my house. Which was a bit depressing. On the plus side, the queue to the toilet was impressively short."

DURING the bells, Anne McCrae and her husband discussed what would improve their relationship, going forward into 2022.

"We should learn something new, like a foreign language or a musical instrument," said Anne.

"Well, there is something . . ." mused her husband.

Anne eagerly leaned forward to discover what esoteric and invaluable branch of knowledge her hubby wished to acquire.

"What I'd love to learn," he said, "is which of our neighbours never puts the bins out in our block of flats."

MANY of our readers persevere with a post-festivities health kick, which tends to last as long as it takes to read this story.

Pamela Taylor gets in touch to say: "I've realised the problem isn't what I eat between Christmas and New Year. It's what I eat between New Year and Christmas."

OPTIMISTIC Scottish broadcaster Catriona Shearer has big plans for the year ahead:

Write a book.
Host own show on radio and TV.
Lose the three stones gained since first lockdown.
Be more realistic.

ON January the First, reader Sue Stanley asked her 86-year-old father if he wanted anything from the shops. He replied: "When I was younger I never thought I'd see the day when men walked on the moon and you could buy spuds on New Year's Day. We truly live in remarkable times."

MANY people's New Year resolution is to undertake a "dry January", meaning they'll quit tippling for a month. "I'm definitely not fully off it, but I'll cut down," reveals Glasgow actor Neil John Gibson, who believes it's better to merely restrain revelry and have a "moist January".

"I CHANGED the graphic display on my TV to 1366 x 766," says reader Pete Kennedy. "It's my New Year resolution."

OUR readers continue bragging about their New Year resolutions. "I'm writing a book about hurricanes and tornadoes," boasts Iain Miller. "At present it's only in draft form."

ANOTHER unusual New Year resolution. "I've decided to delete all the German people I know from my phone," says Robert Bartlett. "Now it's Hans-Free."

19

Some Closing Words from the Diary's Resident Guru

FOR the final time in this year's bumper Diary book we have asked our revered Editor to give a State of the Nation address. Though when we visited the boss-man in his office we realised that the state of his suit was in greater disrepair than the British nation could ever be.

We're not trying to say that he's a dishevelled sort of chap. It's just that he has been to several fancy dress parties as Worzel Gummidge, yet never felt the need to visit a costume shop first.

However, you certainly can't accuse our Editor of having a scruffy prose style.

Actually, you probably could. But he wouldn't take a blind bit of notice. He'd be too busy chasing the crows in the office carpark . . .

YOU could say that things just kept getting bigger for Simon Dee, the iconic 1960s chat show host. Especially when it came to the vehicles in which he motored round London.

Most famously there was the Aston Martin, driven along the King's Road by his secretary, Simon in the passenger seat, chic as a Siamese cat.

Later came a London bus. Dee was no longer in the passenger seat. Now he was the driver.

It wasn't only the vehicles that got larger. His debts increased, too. He ended up spending twenty-eight days in Pentonville Prison for non-payment of rates on his Chelsea home.

One thing that didn't get bigger was Dee's career. After a brief period in the spotlight he sank without a trace. (Unless you were one of the passengers on his bus.)

Fame proved a fickle mistress. For one ecstatic afternoon she flirted coquettishly, gave Simon a glancing peck on the cheek, then sashayed off to find a more enticing beau to keep her company through the night.

The reason I find myself thinking about the late Simon Dee is that he must have been one of the last people in Britain to find fame, then to lose it.

When people become famous nowadays, it sticks to them like chewing gum attached to the sole of a Manolo Blahnik heel.

Andy Warhol claimed that one day everyone will be famous for fifteen minutes. The reality is far worse. We're getting to a point of societal saturation, when nearly everyone will be famous . . . forever.

This year a fresh batch of non-entities evolved into entities, courtesy of ITV2 reality show *Love Island*. The programme has now concluded, but don't expect any of the contestants to drive you into Glasgow city centre on a double-decker.

No, they'll cling to the showbiz lifestyle with the tenacious desperation of a toupee hugging the contours of Frank Sinatra's skull.

Big Brother, the granddaddy of reality shows, is being exhumed from its tomb, and returns to TV screens next year, supplying yet more talentless famous folk.

Meanwhile, the Kardashians, Rebekah Vardy, David Beckham – and way too many social influencers – continue desperately vying for non-famous people's attention. But, alas, the non-famous people are too busy becoming famous to care.

The glut of meaningless glitz continues. Eventually there will only be one lonely person left in the UK who isn't a celebrity.

As he waits in the self-service queue in ALDI, a mob of celebs will surround him, pleading with him to "like" their Twitter feeds.

Breaking free of their needy clutches, he'll race homewards with his shopping bags, the mob close behind, screeching: "Have you listened to our latest podcast? Seen our recent TikTok video? Coming to our charity football match?"

With a sigh of relief he'll slam, bolt and double-bolt his front door, locking out all that hideous glamour.

Safe! At last. Or so he thinks.

Then he hears a voice behind him: "Squawk!" shrieks his pet parrot from its diamond-encrusted cage. "I take it you'll be wanting my autograph . . ."

20

The Endorphin Rush of Underpasses

The UK celebrated the Queen's Platinum Jubilee this year. Festivities in England involved flag waving, cap doffing and forelock tugging.

In Scotland we preferred eye rolling, tongue tutting and fist shaking.

They're much the same things, really. Which is why the United Kingdom is such a harmonious group of nations.

With the Jubilee in full swing, literary afficionados began demanding a similar celebration to commemorate the auspicious date when *The Herald* Diary was first published.

Unfortunately a problem was quickly identified. We weren't sure when we were launched, for the Diary's roots are ancient, stretching back further than human memory.

Mysterious daubs were once discovered in the stone-walled

cellar of a Sauchiehall Street watering hole. These rough-hewn scrawls transpired to represent Cro-Magnon man getting up to all manner of amusing hijinks.

Eminent archaeologists – by which we mean the boozers in the upstairs pub – concluded that the images must be ancient examples of the Diary vignette.

Near the pictures were scribbled antiquated anecdotes and palaeolithic puns.

All of this artistry was undoubtedly compiled by the very first *Herald* Diarist, a truly cultured caveman.

Regrettably we don't have any of that chap's musings to publish in the following chapter. Though hopefully we can entice you with some equally timeless tales . . .

"I ONLY recently discovered Albert Einstein was a real person," says reader Laura Jones. "All this time I thought he was only a theoretical physicist."

YET again social media gets to the crux of the matter, with a student at Edinburgh Napier University explaining on Twitter: "I don't support the monarchy whatsoever, but today I witnessed someone calling the Platinum Jubilee the 'Platty Jubes', and I think it has to be the best thing that's come out of it."

A READER received a postcard from friends who are enjoying a road trip in the USA. It was date stamped September 23.

"Given that it took approximately ten weeks to get to me," says our reader, "I thought it was somewhat ironic that my chums sent it from a place in South Dakota called Rapid City."

MULLING over how to become more prosperous in the year ahead, Charles Davies has come to a decision. "I'm opening an Elvis-themed steak restaurant in Glasgow," he says. "For people who love meat tender."

MARRIAGE truly is the tender trap. Russell Smith from Largs recalls a couple, wed for sixty years, who declared proudly that they had never contemplated divorce.

Murder? Certainly.

But never divorce.

WE feel it necessary to file the following story under the category of . . . only in Glasgow.

The daughter of reader Donald Macdonald from Dumfries was shopping in the Dear Green Place when she overheard the following exchange.

Shop Assistant: That's £10.99 please. You get the banter for free.

Customer: Oh aye, and do I get money off for the cheek?

WE previously mentioned in this chapter that someone was overheard referring to the Platinum Jubilee by the jaunty soubriquet 'Platty Jubes'. We now discover that this is fast becoming a trend in these lands, though not everybody is delighted about this unexpected evolution in the Scots language.

Inverness-based playwright Jack MacGregor grumbles: "Platty Jubes sounds like a nineteenth-century euphemism for dysentery."

POLITICAL denials are an art form, as a certain Downing Street Christmas party made clear.

Reader Stuart Swanston recalls the late 1980s, when he persuaded his local MP to ask the Secretary of State about a nuclear weapons convoy that Stuart claimed he had spotted in Edinburgh's morning rush hour traffic, on the very day the local council declared itself a nuclear free zone.

The following response arrived from the Minister for Supply at the MoD: "In reply to your constituent's recently expressed concerns, Her Majesty's Government can neither confirm nor deny the existence of 'nuclear weapons convoys'. But I can assure your constituent that if such convoys existed they would be safe."

A QUESTION straight out of the Wild West from reader Marvin Sutherland, who says: "If you wear cowboy clothes, are you ranch dressing?"

AN inspirational thought from reader Scott Benton, who says: "The only thing that flat-earthers have to fear . . . is sphere itself."

THE Diary tends to focus an unfair amount of attention on Scotland's major cities. Though we belatedly realise that we should also highlight activities occurring in rural parts of the country.

Alan Walker from Carradale sends us a recent edition of the *Campbeltown Courier*, which excitedly reports that a forty-nine-year-old man was issued with a recorded police warning after stealing a snooker chalk cube from the Commercial Inn.

Unfortunately the newspaper article provides no further details, though the Diary is anxious to discover if the criminal mastermind had any accomplices, and whether the heist was long in the planning.

Surely a Hollywood blockbuster must be filmed, based on this thrilling escapade . . .

ALWAYS first with a Royal exclusive, the Diary revealed earlier in this chapter that in Scotland the Queen's Platinum Jubilee is being referred to by many insolent commoners as the Platty Jubes.

We're attempting to find out if Her Maj has been made aware of this treasonous state of affairs, and have been on the blower to our main Palace contact, a gregarious Corgi called Chatty Dave.

Unfortunately Dave's not barking. In other words, he's keeping mum about ma'am.

Though we have discovered that an increasing number of people are uncomfortable with the Platty Jubes terminology.

For we learn of one chap who thinks it sounds like the sort of disease that is transmitted in the boudoir by a rascally bloke with a roving eye, leading to the complaint: "I broke up with him after he gave me platty jubes."

THE NHS is stretched at present, though it seems that you can still get highly specialised treatment when required. An eighty-seven-year-old neighbour of Norma Gibb confided that she had been given an enigma during a recent hospital visit.

Norma was baffled as to what this meant, and speculated that perhaps the woman had been given a 500 piece jigsaw to complete on the operating table, to take her mind off the medical ministrations.

Having mulled it over for some time, our reader finally got

to the "bottom" of the mystery when she concluded that the woman must have received an enema.

A WHILE ago Gilbert MacKay from Newton Mearns found himself working amongst the good folk of Bury.

When asked, "What's the way to Oldham?" they would invariably reply:

"Some 'old 'em this way, some 'old 'em that way."

DECIDING to indulge in some weekday shopping, Bob Wallace from Pollokshields found himself on Buchanan Street one morning. "I could hardly move for people working from home," he reports.

A CHUM of Robin Gilmour from Milngavie was loading the conveyor belt in the Port Glasgow M&S. This chap, who is eighty-seven years old, found himself begging the pardon of the two ladies behind him for his slight tardiness.

"Humble apologies, ladies," said he. "But my wife broke two of her ribs recently, and as you can gather, I'm new to this game."

One of the ladies immediately pulled her pal's sleeve, and said with barely supressed ardour: "Mags, see him? I'm lookin' for wan like that."

CONTEMPLATIVE reader Dan Milne points out: "You can never do all of your laundry at once, unless you are entirely naked."

HIGH school English teacher Mary Chalmers was explaining the plot of *Hamlet* to a group of students in Motherwell who had never previously read or watched a play written by the Bard.

One eager young scholar piped up from the back of the classroom: "So hings just keep gettin' worser and worser for this Hamlet guy? Sounds like the plot of *The Gruffalo*."

SCOTLAND has given the world many great inventions. The bicycle. Television. Penicillin.

Anybody who has ever ridden on a tandem with a TV balanced on the handlebars, while a doctor perches on the back-saddle, administering a jab of antibiotics, has our nation to thank for the experience.

But will we rest on our laurels? Never!

For as we recently mentioned, Scotland has invented an exciting new terminology to denote the Queen's Platinum Jubilee . . . Platty Jubes.

Even the English are taking up the phrase, though it seems it is not without controversy, for Edinburgh novelist Ross McCleary has noted that some philistines are spelling it incorrectly.

"Platty Jubes, not Platty Joobs," roars Ross. "Come on, people, have some self-respect."

ANALYSING our tale about the chap issued with a recorded police warning for stealing a snooker chalk cube from a local inn, reader Finlay Buchanan says: "I wonder if the police told the bloke he was under a rest?"

STROLLING along Glasgow's Buchanan Street, reader Simon Coulson spotted one of those doom-mongering street preachers who like to lecture passing shoppers about the world going to hell in a handcart. (Which is obviously inaccurate information. The world would never fit in a handcart. Plus the wheels on your average handcart are too shoogly to get anywhere near the flaming gates of Hades.)

This street preacher was complaining about the cruel tyrants who rule large swathes of the planet. Which led him to screech at the top of his voice: "Down with dictation!"

Our reader says: "I'm guessing the bloke meant 'down with dictatorship'. Though any office secretary who happened to be passing would probably have preferred his chosen phrasing."

MEDICALLY minded Richard Davis from Vienna once worked as a social worker in the old Southern General Hospital, where an old woman informed him she had a hysterical rectum.

Understandably confused, Richard checked her medical records and discovered she had in fact been given a . . . hysterectomy.

STEVEN Spielberg's version of *West Side Story* was showing in cinemas a while back. A similar tale of star-cross'd lovers played out in Shawlands, in what the Diary had no choice but to label . . . South Side Story.

Reader Jan Bracey was walking behind two girls in school uniform, when she heard one say to the other: "So obviously am no gonnie let a boy spit oan me. So I pit a pencil in his hair, then he goes an tells the teacher . . ."

Our reader was understandably entranced. "Ain't young love grand?" she sighs.

AN intrigued reader overheard two women in an Ayr shop discussing the Omicron variant outbreak and the need to restrict socialising.

Said one to the other: "If they want us to stay in the hoose at night, they need tae stop pittin' *Mrs Brown's Boys* oan the telly."

PHILOSOPHICAL reader Bert Lawrenson points out: "We brush our teeth with hair on a stick and brush our hair with teeth on a stick."

OUR mention of *West Side Story* reminds Douglas McLeod from Newlands of a conversation with some pals. The chat on such occasions is often knowledgably focused on football and indie music, but the gang's weak grasp of musical theatre was displayed when one chap mentioned he and his wife had visited London to see *Hamilton*.

There was a moment of collective puzzlement, until one chap responded: "What? The Accies?"

THE Diary team are sensitive to a fault. You are unlikely to find us in the queue for the latest Tom Cruise aeronautical blockbuster. We'd much rather sit at home, a box of scented tissues on our knees, as we leak tears of anguish watching a classic Bette Davis weepie on the telly.

Being gentle souls, we also hate to witness bullying, especially the bullying of someone as vulnerable as an international sex symbol and rock god.

So you can understand our concern when we discovered that Rod Stewart was being mercilessly mocked for his performance of "Sweet Caroline" at the Party at the Palace concert to celebrate the Platty Jubes.

We have now taken the difficult decision to repeat one of the nasty comments aimed at the Celtic-mad crooner, hoping to shame the culprit into future silence.

So it's more with sorrow than anger that we quote one chap on social media, who snickered: "Can someone send in a locksmith? Rod Stewart needs a key change."

A WHILE ago reader Jake Morgan was forced to endure a lecture from his accountancy firm boss, who pompously parroted the tiresome cliché to a room of office workers that: "There is no 'I' in team."

The chap sitting next to Jake whispered to him with a wink: "Mibbe there's no 'I' in team. But there's five of 'em in individual brilliance."

AN elderly lady was overheard exchanging polite chit-chat with the driver as she got on a Whitecraigs bus. "It's a lovely crisp morning," said the woman.

"Aye," agreed the driver, perhaps not quite understanding. "I've had two packs already."

OBSERVANT Iain Mills from Largs notes that the new head of the Port Glasgow shipyard, Ferguson Marine, is the appropriately monikered . . . David Tydeman.

CONVIVIAL Diary correspondent Finlay Buchanan was at a Platty Jubes street party where attendees were invited to participate in a quiz featuring regal anagrams. One jumbled-up phrase was "alloys ear".

A triumphant Finlay was just about to shout out the words

"loyal a**e", when a fellow team member spoiled his fun by pointing out that the correct answer was "royal seal".

ENJOYING the boozy badinage in a bustling hostelry in Glasgow's East End, reader Rab Cameron heard a chap at the bar say to the grumpy girl standing next to him: "C'moan, doll. You know I'd go tae the end o' the earth fir ye."

To which the lady in question sweetly responded: "Gid idea. An' once ye get there, wid ye mind stayin' put?"

THE wonderful thing about social media is that it inspires so many profound and penetrating conversations. For example, the Diary stumbled upon a discussion about the splendours of town planning in Scotland, with one chap saying: "God, I love a good underpass. Grew up with them as a kid and still prefer them to crossing the road. The smell, the fear, the graffiti and the endorphin rush of coming out the other side unscathed."

CULINARY minded reader Melinda Hodges gets in touch to say: "If most spiders were as big as lobsters, people would eat them in posh restaurants and get charged an arm and a leg . . . or four arms and four legs, perhaps."

FORGING a successful career in this current era of economic uncertainty can be difficult. Reader Harvey Benjamin says: "My boss always laughed at my jokes when I was in the office. But when lockdown started he never laughed at them during Zoom chats."

Harvey enquired why this was the case. His boss replied: "Because your jokes aren't remotely funny."

MATHEMATICALLY minded reader Ian Noble tells us: "4/3 people don't understand fractions."

WE mentioned in the Christmas chapter of this book that in some quarters a buffet meal is known as a "picky tea". Reader Debbie Meehan tells us that her family called this style of dining a "kick at the cat and a run round the table."

"I've no idea why," adds Debbie. "We didn't even have a cat."

A MATHEMATICALLY minded reader informed us earlier in this chapter that 4/3 of people don't understand fractions.

"I say that's improper," argues Brian Logan from Glasgow.

THE Diary always appreciates when our readers provide us with profound linguistic analysis. "The final four letters in the word 'queue' aren't silent," says Mandy Nicholson. "They're just patiently waiting their turn."

OUR prodigiously intelligent readers have been dazzling us in this chapter with their wise thoughts on mathematics. Bob Metcalf gets in touch to point out that "spelling the word 'three' with only two e's is a missed opportunity".

21

The Chap Who Fell in Love with Saliva

AS we mentioned previously, the Diary became obsessed with the Tory leadership race in 2022.

Eventually most of the combatants were ejected from the contest, leaving only two politicians with hope of victory.

First there was Rishi Sunak, with all the magnetic intensity of a trainee call-centre manager who has his very own cubicle to work in. The kind of chap who emphasises his devil-may-care streak by loosening his tie on Friday afternoons, and nabbing an extra Caramel Log from the communal biscuit tin in the staff canteen.

Rival candidate Liz Truss had even less oomph, though she made up for her shortcomings with an impressive ability to deliver a speech as though reciting a haiku written entirely in Morse code.

The following chapter also has its fair share of charismatic personalities, so brace yourselves for rather a lot of drama.

Though regrettably we can't promise you any Caramel Logs . . .

IT is an X-Rated era we are living through. Reader Michael Deeming says: "My sixteen-year-old son persuaded me to watch the Netflix show *Sex Education* with him. Despite the risqué title, he assured me it was a typical teenage drama series, though it turned out to be a mixture of *Grange Hill* and *Debbie Does Dallas*."

Our outraged reader adds: "Bring back Bill and Ben *The Flowerpot Men*. They may have appeared on TV in skimpy attire, but at least they had their modesty hidden behind earthenware."

CONCERNED reader John Delaney from Lochwinnoch read online that the AGM for Lurpak shareholders has been cancelled due to covid. "There were fears it would become a super-spreader event," he says.

DURING her student years reader Joanna Holden worked a range of part-time jobs, including waitressing in a grubby restaurant in Glasgow's south side. She recalls her first day serving tables, when a colleague said to her: "Don't hold out on making any extra cash on top of your wages. The only tip you'll get in here is the kitchen."

FEMALE wisdom at its finest. Reader Clive Dawson was on a train when he overheard one middle-aged lady say to another: "So how are you feeling nowadays?"

"Much better," replied her chum, "now that I'm in denial."

LOVE, Glesga style. Reader Roger Stewart had a pal who once got chatting to a girl in Glasgow's fabled Cleopatra's nightclub.

"You're single. I'm single. We both know what that means," sizzled this suave fellow.

"Aye," replied the girl. "Naebody wants us."

THE above tale reminds John Hart of the chap who said to a young lady at the dancing: "Where are you going for your holidays?"

Just about breaking through the loud music, he heard her reply: "Naples."

"Ah, Naples," sighed the chap. "The city of romance! Such beautiful sunshine . . ."

"Naw," corrected the young lady, firmly. "I said, 'Nae place.'"

OBSERVANT reader Gordon McRae spotted a statement in a newspaper which read: "30 minutes' exercise won't counteract sitting all day, but light movement helps."

"So I tried moving my desk lamp a couple of times, but didn't feel any great benefit," shrugs Gordon.

NEWS just in from reader Brian Thomas, who says. "A mummy covered in chocolate and nuts has been discovered in Egypt. Archaeologists believe it may be Pharaoh Rocher."

THE above mention of a popular snack puts John Ferguson from Milngavie in a suspicious mood.

"Is it just me," he says, "or are there no Ferrero Rocher adverts on anymore?"

The Diary decided to discover if this is indeed the case, and why it may have happened. Our intrepid team of investigative reporters rushed to the local corner shop to purchase as many Ferrero Rocher as we could carry, before undertaking some scientific analysis

Intriguingly, we discovered that the treat, unwrapped from its gold foil, is ball shaped with little spikes coating its surface. In other words, it looks like an enlarged version of the covid atom.

So perhaps Nicola Sturgeon banned Ferrero adverts to prevent confused TV viewers jumping to the conclusion that there is a delicious new variant of covid.

Unfortunately the Diary team couldn't proceed any further in its investigation.

For the evidence we had so painstakingly accrued inexplicably vanished, while the majority of our reporters stumbled off home with tummy ache.

YEARS ago, reader Martin Coe's boss asked him why he only seemed to get sick on weekdays. "Must be my weekend immune system," he replied.

(And, no, Martin didn't last long in the job.)

OBSERVANT reader Scott Simpson notes that Glasgow's electric buses are manufactured by Yutong.

"Bet they wouldn't have written that on the back of the local vehicles in the fifties and sixties," chuckles Scott.

SHOPAHOLIC reader Ken Chandler decided to buy coconut shampoo. "Though when I got home," he sighs, "I realised I didn't have a coconut."

AN academic has been using social media to further her knowledge of a previously underexamined area of anthropological scholarship.

"Doing my dissertation on the Tennent's Lager Lovelies campaign," reveals Caitlin McCabe on Twitter, before requesting that her followers complete a survey on the ladies in question.

Our readers may recall that the Lager Lovelies were attractive young women whose scantily clad bodies decorated cans of Tennent's back in the Neanderthal epoch of beer imbibing. A time before feminist entreaties won the day with the booze-guzzling public.

It seems that this long ago era isn't quite so long ago as we assumed, for one respondent answers Caitlin's request by drooling: "Good looking women on beer! What's not to like?"

"BINMEN are the opposite of postmen," claims reader Eric Hamilton. "Because binmen take the junk away from your house."

WHEN reader Rob Baker visited Czechoslovakia many years ago he was intrigued by the advertising slogan used to promote the country's own brand of cola, which was: "Good or weird?"

Says Rob: "I suppose some people may have concluded it was both. The sort of people who like haggis, for instance."

HISTORICALLY minded reader Murray Garner says: "The worst thing about being called Spartacus is that someone else will always get your taxi."

A BOOZE-IMBIBING reader points out that the principle investor of the new Ardgowan whisky distillery at Inverclyde is the appropriately named . . . Roland Grain.

A FRIEND of Robin Gilmour from Milngavie suffered a tragic loss after his wife instructed him to remove a twelve-pack of beer from the fridge which was taking up too much space.

Winter conditions outside resembled the fridge, so the booze was transferred to the back doorstep.

When the door was opened the following morning the beer had vanished. Replacing it was a pencilled note jammed in a milk bottle, which read: "Our favourite customer . . . thanks! The binmen."

WE continue reminiscing about those scantily clad females known as the Tennent's Lager Lovelies.

Michael Smith recalls being on a train leaving Glasgow's High Street station when he spotted some gents who were clearly getting a thrill out of ogling the beer cans in their possession.

"I've got Amanda!" gulped one chap.

"I've got Brenda!" gasped another.

The next fellow, who happened to be dribbling from his mouth, shrieked: "I've got Saliva!"

(The lady portrayed on the side of his can turned out to be Sylvia, though we're still not convinced that's what he meant to say . . .)

SCOTIA'S native gourmands have been known to indulge in deep-fried pizza and haggis fritters. It seems that our English chums also enjoy deliciously deranged dishes, for a swanky

London noshery has been boasting about the stuffed duck neck on its menu.

An image posted on the restaurant's Instagram shows the amputated neck plonked on a plate, with the unfortunate fowl's head still attached.

Reader Ken Roberts says: "Complaining about the bill at the end of a meal has never been so apt."

WATCHING TV, Peter Niven from the Isle of Bute found himself intrigued by a programme extolling the virtues of a diet based on vegetables and pulses.

What most fascinated our reader was the home economist working on the show, who was named . . . Anita Bean.

FORMER Labour MP Sir Brian Donohoe gets in touch to marvel at the latest instruction from Glasgow Health Board, who advise people to "walk like a penguin" in order to avoid slipping in icy conditions.

The Diary would like more information before complying with this request.

For starters, which type of penguin should we be imitating, Batman's portly nemesis or the crunchy biscuit?

A BUSINESS query from reader Philip Rushton, who says: "Why don't Selfridges sell fridges?"

22

Wilde Cats and Merciless Lawnmowers

WE were sad to hear in August that the model Jerry Hall had divorced Rupert Murdoch, after six years of marriage.

Murdoch is, of course, a famous media magnate. We're not entirely sure what a magnate is, but it's probably similar to a magnet, which means that little chunks of metal, such as pound coins, are attracted to Murdoch's person, going someway to explaining why he's so rich.

Jerry has now put the kibosh on a chunk of that dosh, as she allegedly walked off with $305 million in the divorce settlement, along with at least three houses the couple owned. (None of them being a high flat in Easterhouse, we're guessing.)

Jerry is probably grief-stricken that her latest relationship failed, and she'll no doubt use some of those dollar bills that she's freshly accrued to wipe away the tears of anguish.

Another way she can cheer herself up is by perusing the following chapter.

We can't give our readers piles of cash. But at least we provide a mountain of laughs . . .

BURNS Night is all about tradition. Though occasionally something new is brought to the party . . .

Businessman David Jackson from Newton Mearns recalls spending one such celebration in a hotel where he was hosting a trade delegation from Romania.

The Eastern Europeans had been promised a spectacular feast to celebrate the birthday of Scotland's most famous poet. They were told that they would savour exotic treats such as they had never indulged in before, including haggis and After Eight mints.

As the festivities commenced, David glanced at one of the Romanians and witnessed a sight that chilled him to the very marrow.

The delegate was smearing a lump of haggis on an After Eight, which he was using like a cracker.

His fellow Romanians nodded in approval, and did likewise.

The meal was not a roaring success.

THE daughter-in-law of Sandy Macdonald from Paisley went to a performance of *The Importance of Being Earnest.* Inspired by the characters on stage, she has now decided that any pet cats she owns in the future will be named Algernon and Ernest.

Says Sandy: "I wonder, will they be wilde cats?"

KINDLY reader Dave Leitch offered a visiting pal an apple. "But he told me he preferred pears," says Dave. "So I gave him another apple."

"MY helium addiction is out of control," admits reader Matthew Brown. "But no one is taking my cry for help seriously."

IN the above story a concerned reader mentioned his addiction to helium. Gordon Casely sufferers from the same condition. "But I continue to rise with the challenge," he says.

THERE will be a lot less to chew on for contemporary viewers of classic Scottish sketch show *Chewin' The Fat*.

The BBC have removed certain scenes, fearing they might offend modern sensibilities.

The Diary is curious to know what other programmes will face the snippety-snip from the Beeb's censorious scissor waggers.

"I predict they'll tackle the 1970s sitcom about sustainable living, *The Good Life*," says reader Emma Trimble. "Especially those episodes where Tom Good brandishes a sharp blade, with clear intent to harm."

Emma adds: "Modern audiences would be appalled to witness Tom ripping up a poor, defenceless lawn with his merciless lawnmower."

THE Diary continues to shine a light on the curious phenomenon of people whose monikers provide a quirky commentary on their chosen profession.

Browsing an Australian newspaper, Lachlan Bradley stumbled across an article about the New South Wales health officer, who has signed an amendment to the Public Health Act to "Prohibit singing and dancing by persons attending music festivals".

And the name of this rather puritanical and authoritarian dignitary?

Kerry Chant.

ANOTHER person with a strangely appropriate name. Reader Brian Chrystal was genuinely sorry to hear about the

Devonshire chap whose pet ducks were put down after catching bird flu.

Though he also notes that the unfortunate fellow is named Alan Gosling.

OBSERVANT David Donaldson has noticed an unusual sound in Glasgow's Hyndland – the hooting of an owl.

"You can tell it's not a native of the West End," he says, "because it goes 'To-who' instead of 'To-whom.'"

A MEDIC with a morbid moniker. Fraser Kelly, who is based in Manila in the Philippines, says: "When I was training at the Western Infirmary there was a new doc called Doctor Death in the ward. He pronounced it dee-ath. Though that didn't reassure the patients."

A FILTHY story. Grant MacKenzie from Bearsden recalls his wife's valiant attempt to toilet train one of their children.

On one occasion Grant returned home from work to be greeted in the hall by the nappyless youth, proudly announcing that he had: "Done a poo!"

Not wishing to dampen his enthusiasm, our reader heartily congratulated the wee fella, then enquired where, specifically, he had performed this deed.

"In my hand!" reported the child triumphantly, proffering his unclenched fist.

FED up with footy, gleekit-eyed when it comes to golf, the Diary is keen to find a thrilling new sport to follow. Which is why we're delighted to learn that the World Tattie Scone Championships are being staged at Nairn Community & Arts Centre.

No expense has been spared, for competitors will each be provided with mashed potato and their very own spatula.

Alas, the Diary is grievously disappointed to learn that for their special ingredient, those same competitors are banned from adding a dash of booze.

(Sigh. Guess we'll have to go back to pretending to enjoy kickyball . . .)

MUSIC FAN Stewart Daniels from Cairneyhill was listening to his car radio, when Aretha Franklin's 1985 hit "Who's Zoomin' Who?" started playing.

At which point Stewart realised that not only was Aretha a fairly decent soul singer.

She was also an advanced economic thinker when it came to predicting the future of office work.

THERE was a satisfying conclusion to this year's *Eurovision Song Contest*. Some lank-haired chap from the UK – looking like Thor impersonating a Bee Gee impersonating Thor – came second, and beleaguered Ukraine bagged victory. (We're sure they would have preferred peace within their sovereign borders, but winning a camp singing competition will have to do for now.)

The majority of the night was, inevitably, a showcase for silly, surreal and so-so singing . . . . so-so being a synonym for absolute tosh.

Understanding all this, Harry Shaw from Airdrie says: "I think there's someone with a sense of humour in scheduling at the BBC. Anyone wanting to avoid Eurovision on BBC1 on Saturday night had the perfect alternative on BBC2 . . . *Far from the Madding Crowd.*"

A WHILE ago an acquaintance of Thorfinn Johnston from Stromness decided to set up a new business in Kirkwall. Wanting to reflect Orkney's Viking heritage, she was keen to name her hairdressing salon after the Norse god of beauty.

She wisely sought another solution when her research uncovered the name of this particular deity . . . Balder.

ONE Saturday evening Stranraer taxi driver Alastair Clark had the pleasure of picking up two latter-day likely lads. While waiting for their lift to arrive, they had spent some quality time in the taxi office, which is entirely staffed by female dispatchers.

This led to the following animated conversation in the backseat of the cab . . .

Likely Lad 1: See me? Those gurls don't know what hit them. (proud) I was seducing them!

Likely Lad 2: (arch aside to taxi driver) His hips need chained!

Likely Lad 1: (suave, like a Stranraer David Niven) Aye, when we left, they knew they'd been seducted.

SOCIAL media continues to be the ideal forum for serious, thoughtful conversations. For example, we were impressed by a young Glasgow lady named Gemma who was clearly in a deeply contemplative mood when she took to Twitter to ask: "See when they cook pigeon on *MasterChef*, is it just like a pigeon you get in Central Station, or do you get fancy ones?"

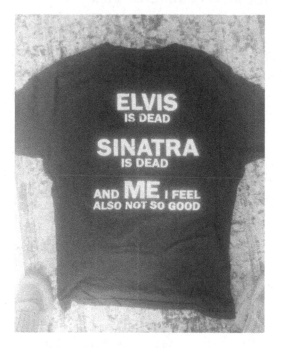

THE above philosophical speculation from Gemma inspired one of her Twitter pals to provide an answer, stating: "They send Gregg Wallace out to walk the streets with a big net."

ISLAND-HOPPING reader David Donaldson spent time on Mull recently, and tells us that after a two-year hiatus the local Duck Race has triumphantly returned, with a total of 117 ducks taking part.

David reports that the race was won by no. 25, who went by the name of "A Very Tasty Dinner".

Unfortunately our sporting correspondent also discovered that the competitors were all plastic ducks, manipulated by gleeful children prodding them along the water with sticks.

Plastic ducks in a competitive duck race?! The Diary is scandalised. Surely this is as bad as any sneaky steroid usage in the Olympic Games.

The people of Mull (and their dastardly duckies) should be thoroughly ashamed of themselves — it's time to call fowl on fake waterfowl.

MOST sensible newspaper columnists decry the demon drink. The Diary, however, has a more circumspect attitude towards alcohol.

This is partially because in our office we have not yet adapted to computer technology and still rely on ancient, rusty typewriters, which can only be lubricated by a generous application of single malt whisky each morning, which is poured into the inner workings of the machinery.

Single malts are expensive, of course, so we once tried drizzling cans of Special Brew over our typewriter keys, instead. Unfortunately the copy produced that day turned out to be unsettlingly tabloid, with references to soap opera plot lines and the amorous activities of footballers.

Meanwhile, our readers have been confessing that they share our interest in booze. Gordon Berry from Ayr recalls reading that binge drinkers are getting younger, which made him think to himself: "If that's what it takes to get younger, I'll give it a go."

THE Diary deems it necessary to inform our readers about the theft of Michelangelo's painting *Leda and the Swan*, back in the 1530s. (As ever we're topical, and first with an art heist scoop.)

Alas, the painting has never been recovered.

We now discover that another work of rare and timeless beauty has been pilfered, this time closer to home.

For we hear that Larry the Lobster, a lifelike model of a crustacean that usually enjoys pride of place in North Queensferry eatery The Wee Restaurant, has been nabbed, most likely by a customer.

The Diary demands Larry's swift return, and asks the readers of this book to keep their eyes peeled for a shady figure carrying a fake lobster in one hand ... and perhaps a pretty picture of a swan in the other hand.

(Now that WOULD be a result.)

WE'RE disappointed that the *Batgirl* movie filmed in Glasgow some months ago will not be shown on any media platform.

So it won't be on a cinema screen, a TV screen or any other screen you care to mention. And that includes the screen-door that opens from your greenhouse onto the back garden.

Why was the bat belle given the bullet? Who knows? Maybe the Joker has taken over as CEO at Warner Bros, the studio who made the axed flick.

Meanwhile, wannabe movie mogul David Donaldson suggests that Glasgow should be given the outtakes from the film, so that we can cobble together a work of unsurpassed genius for local consumption.

And what would this magnum opus be called?

"Bamgirl," suggests our resident auteur. "Or perhaps Senga the Avenga."

FORMER mafia boss Michael Franzese has been enjoying the sights in Glasgow while on a speaking tour of the UK.

In 1986 *Vanity Fair* magazine named Michael one of the biggest money earners in the mob since Al Capone. So he was obviously a rather successful chap in his highly specialised line of work.

Alas, we do not think he would be equally successful as a Glasgow tour guide, if he was so inclined to follow such a career path.

Strolling on Buchanan Steet, Michael pointed excitedly, and said: "That's Nelson Mandela Plaza."

The Diary assumes he meant Nelson Mandela Place, though we certainly won't be correcting him.

We've seen too many business-instruction videos starring Al Pacino and Robert De Niro to be so cheeky . . .

23

Bow Down to Your
Seagull Overlords

WE surmise that most Diary aficionados will initially pick up this book during the Yuletide season, that magical time when the Scottish weather gods flex their pecs and strut around, showing off their bulging six-packs.

In other words, brace yourself for oodles of snow, hail, sleet, rain, wind, (a wee bit of sarcastic sunshine) then more snow, hail, sleet, rain etc.

And that's just the first five minutes of every single day, when the weather gods are still in the process of waking up, and haven't yet reached peak levels of diabolical malevolence.

So what should one do in such circumstances?

Batten down the hatches, of course. And if you haven't got any hatches (or battens) Sellotape the curtains shut instead.

Now enjoy a few toasty-warm chuckles, courtesy of the following chapter, which contains several tales celebrating the delights of Scottish summer.

(Yup, there really was such a thing in 2022, hard as it is to believe.)

THE Diary team is based in Glasgow, though we have embedded spies in every major location in the world.

For example, there's a chap reporting from the peak of Mount Everest, where he's been stationed for decades, though he rarely telegraphs us any topical stories.

In his last message, wired seven months ago, he merely said: "Rather chilly up here. Permission to come home?"

We nixed that suggestion, though posted him a bobble hat.

Meanwhile, Diary correspondent Graham Sutherland reports from enemy territory. (Edinburgh, of course.)

At General Register House, Princes Street, he spots a statue of Wellington with a traffic cone on its head, much like the Glasgow original.

This is concept thievery. As outrageous as London building its own Eiffel Tower.

The Diary demands to know who is responsible. Though being conciliatory chaps, we won't punish the culprit, but offer a plum job instead.

For there's a wonderful opportunity just about to open up in our Everest station . . .

IN Dundee city centre Tina Oakes spotted two couples approaching each other.

One of the blokes shouted to the other: "I was waiting for you to call me last Friday."

To which the other chap replied: "Sorry, Jim. A man was in fixing my Virgin."

It was only after a few seconds of utter astonishment that the penny finally dropped, and Tina realised that he just might have been referring to his broadband rather than a broad.

TRUE story. Once upon a time there was a huge, flaming orb whose home was in the sky.

It was called the Sun.

Being a rather snobbish flaming orb, it declined to spend any time hobnobbing with the grey proletariat clouds of

Scotland, instead preferring the high society azure above the Mediterranean.

One unfortunate day in July 2022 the Snobbish Sun mislaid its sat nav, couldn't find its way to Ibiza, and ended up hovering over Alba.

The people of Alba were delighted . . .

No, wait. That last bit isn't true. The people of Alba were discomfited, outraged and terrified, demanding a return of dreich downpours and drookit raincoats.

Though one bold fellow on Scottish social media saw the constructive side, writing: "Advice to current Tory Cabinet Members: treat this weather as a training drill for where you're going to end up."

WE mentioned that Scotland has been enduring a smattering of genuine summer days in July. Even worse have been the sizzling summer nights.

Glasgow comedian and author David Bratchpiece says: "That was one of those sleeps where you learn what it's like to be a slow-cooked chicken."

THE above tale motivates reader Jim Kent to deliver this warning . . .

"IMPORTANT: During the hot weather drink lots of water. TOP TIP: It's fine in frozen form, though you may need to smear it in a whisky lubricant to make it more palatable."

CONNOISSEUR of all things cartoonish, Derek Quinn, says: "It's disappointing that Wile E. Coyote is remembered for his violence, and not for his impeccably realistic paintings of tunnels."

CHIVALRY isn't dead in Scotland. It's merely enjoying a centuries-long snooze.

Strolling with his sister, Robin Gilmour from Milngavie spotted a young couple.

The chap was breezily sauntering along, carrying what seemed to be his birthday card, leaving his female companion to struggle with a full tray of large water bottles.

Robin grinned cheekily at the fellow, then said: "I've always wanted to know what a girl with a six-pack looks like. She's stunning. Happy Birthday!"

The bloke courteously thanked Robin. His companion was too busy hefting her back-breaking bottles to say a thing.

A CULINARY question from foody fan David Crawford. "My wife recently gave me mozzarella balls in a salad," says David. "They were delicious. Can you tell me what other parts of a mozzarella are edible, and if they have the same flavour?"

MORE on those swelteringly hot evenings. Thankfully there's a simple solution to the problem, if it continues to arise throughout the summer. Open the bedroom window.

Though perhaps not.

Glasgow comedian Limmy says: "Everybody listen. I know a lot of yous will have your windows open to let in a breeze, but there's meant to be these guys going about dressed as killer clowns, and they're jumping through open windows with razors. Night."

WE mentioned chivalry not being dead in Scotland. It's merely like the unfortunate black knight in *Monty Python and the Holy Grail*. Sans arms, sans legs; all that remains is a bleeding torso.

Which reminds Robin Gilmour from Milngavie of his aunt and uncle who lived in magical Millport.

Visitors were rare, so on the occasional hot day the mode of dress adopted at home was the one described by anthropologists of leisurewear as "the scuddy".

For health reasons the couple were obliged to vacate their Shangri-La, relocating to a Glasgow flat.

The couple's naturist ways persisted, leading Robin's uncle to ungallantly proclaim one hot day: "We're not in Millport now, dear. So please don't stand at that window letting all the neighbours know I only married you for your money."

WE noted that the warm July weather was panicking the populace, with news anchors predicting imminent Armageddon. Or, more ominously, a shortage of inflatable children's paddling pools in Argos.

Ted Hamilton was in a South Side boozer and heard two blokes discussing the cataclysmic climate.

"It's pure worryin', all this weather we're havin'," said one chap.

"Zat right?" said his pal, adding: "You know what they call this sort of weather in the Costa del Sol?"

The first chap conceded that he didn't.

"Winter," said the pal.

ENTERTAINING advice from reader Dennis Stewart, who says: "A whoopee cushion loaded with gravy adds a hilarious new dimension to a rather tiresome joke."

BROWSING in a Muirend corner shop, reader Arnold Harrison spotted a father with his son, aged about six, talking to the chap behind the till.

The youngster had a fake tattoo displayed on his arm; the type often sported by dashing young fellows with a rebellious streak.

The shopkeeper nervously enquired if the boy was a pirate. The boy assured him he was not.

"Well, since you're all grown-up with that fancy tattoo, why don't you pay for Daddy's groceries?" said the shopkeeper.

The boy responded by thrusting out his tongue and blasting a rip-snorting raspberry.

"Must be a pirate after all," shuddered the shopkeeper.

THERE was an Old Worthy from West Kilbride who had much wisdom to impart regarding the view of Ailsa Craig from the shore at Seamill.

He explained that if you could see Ailsa Craig it was going to rain.

If you couldn't see it, it was already raining.

SOME confusing contemplation from reader Jennifer Pattison, who says: "The opposite of identical is opposite."

HOT weather, continued. Russell Smith from Largs says: "During the previous heatwave I took off all my clothes and opened the windows. Unfortunately some people on the bus objected."

WE mentioned the weather being fair bilin' in these parts. One chap we quoted even compared the outdoor temperature to the fiery pit down below.

And, no, he wasn't referring to England.

Meanwhile, legendary entertainer Andy Cameron gets in touch to usher us away from the Gates of Hades, pointing in the direction of a far more salubrious locale. Our destination is, in fact, the most delightful neighbourhood that has ever existed.

And, no, we don't mean Newton Mearns. We're referring to the Garden of Eden.

Andy tells us the true tale of Adam and Eve's first falling out.

"After a ding-dong barney, Adam stormed off in a huff for a month," says Andy. "On his return, Eve snarled: 'Whit dae you want?' Adam replied: 'Ma leave's up.'"

WE continue analysing the strained relationship between Biblical couples.

We're told that one ominous day in the Garden of Eden, Eve snarled at Adam: "You're having an affair!"

Adam stoutly denied such an indiscretion.

"Yes, you are," countered Eve. "You're missing another rib."

MORE religious ramblings from reader Gordon Casely, who says: "Is it true that Adam and Eve were the first to ignore Apple terms and conditions?"

ON a similar topic ... Reader Nigel Barr says: "As I walk through the valley of the Shadow of Death, I remind myself that you can't always trust Google Maps."

FORMER Labour MP Sir Brian Donohoe tells us that when he was employed by the Hunterston A power station in Ayrshire the spiders found near the reactor were five to six inches in size.

Which is five to six inches larger than any spider has a right to be ...

ON social media Glasgow thespian Alasdair Hankinson expresses his appreciation for the skills of a fellow practitioner of the dramatic arts.

Or perhaps not ...

Says Alasdair: "Just witnessed the most over-egged, focus-pulling death scene I've ever seen an actor perform on a stage. The other two actors were saying some of the most important lines in the play, meanwhile actor X is on the floor shaking, gurgling and gasping all the way through it. Mental."

The Diary demands to know the name of the play, and where it's being staged. For we intend to buy tickets for every performance.

In other words ... Play it again, ham.

SOME basic maths. Cloudless sky + hot sun = paradise. However ... Cloudless sky + hot sun + seagull = hell on earth.

At least that's what Deedee Cuddihy tells us. Our intrepid

correspondent has been hearing from numerous desperate souls who have barely recovered from encounters with the brash, brigand birdies.

One of Deedee's Glasgow chums was attempting to enjoy a two-scoop vanilla ice-cream cone while holidaying in Whitby.

Unfortunately a local varmint of the seagull variety operated a two-scoop swoop and vamoosed with the vanilla.

Deedee has also been notified of a Dumfries seagull who instigated a flapjack attack, while an Ayrshire gull gobbled a hot doughnut.

The Diary suggests the human race should surrender immediately and bow down to our seagull overlords.

Who knows, they may show pity and let us nibble a handful of yummy worms, while they enjoy a hearty repast at the local carvery.

A TRUE tale of teenage torpor. Lisa Byrne from Shawlands asked her sixteen-year-old son to go to the corner shop across the road to pick up groceries.

The lad declined, explaining he was still suffering from symptoms akin to jet lag following a family holiday.

"I wouldn't have minded," says Lisa. "It's just that the family holiday was a weekend in Millport."

THE above mention of a listless youth inspires Russell Smith from Largs to recall: "As a teenager I had a friend who could sleep for a week without a rest."

NOSTALGIC for halcyon days of yore, reader Tony Mellow says: "Truly, there was no better feeling than snapping shut your flip-phone to hang up on someone annoying."

EARLIER in this chapter we reported the terrifying true story of a breed of giant spiders that proliferated near the Hunterston A power station in Ayrshire.

We realise our readers are a delicate tribe, so we won't reveal precisely how massive these arachnids were.

Though we will say that the eight-legged freaks would have come in handy during the 2022 crises in fuel prices. For instead of driving to work, it would be cheaper to saddle-up a Hunterston spider, then gallop the beasty down the M8.

Meanwhile, optimistic reader Brian Chrystal says: "Nuclear power stations can be good for us. A chap fishing on the shore near Torness told me he enjoyed an excellent leg of cod for dinner."

WE'RE discussing the properties of a curious liquid which goes by the name of water. (You may have heard of it. It's very much like whisky, only without the colour, taste and delightful side-effects.)

Reader Joe Knox says: "I was wondering if semi-skimmed water Is H_1O."

A DIARY correspondent recalls the occasion when a wee leary (the chap who sauntered from close to close extinguishing the gas lighting) attempted to board a tramcar during a rainstorm in the Coocaddens.

The lady clippie informed him that he, "Isnae gettin' oan ma caur wi that ladder."

After negotiations ended, the poor fellow was left standing in the downpour, clutching his dinky ladder as the car trundled towards Maryhill.

Understandably outraged, he called to the snippy clippie: "Ach, stick yer caur up yer a**e."

To which the clippie replied: "You dae that wi' yer ladder and ah'll let ye oan ma caur."

THE above story reminds Barrie Crawford of a match at Fir Park. The linesman raised his flag, indicating one of the home players was offside.

An irate Motherwell fan yelled: "Haw, linesman, stick yer flag up yer a**e!"

The linesman duly retorted: "Ah canny. It's fu' o' whustles!"

OUR tale referencing the indomitable ladies who once worked on the local transport system reminds Ritchie Young of his local village station mistress, back in the 1960s.

A large, formidable woman, she would shout as trains arrived at the platform: "A' youse in there for here get oot."

Well-liked by the engine drivers, they often gave her coal for her home fire, which she carried in a large shopping bag.

When she worked late in winter, the village bobby escorted

her home in the dark, not realising his companion was concealing "hot" British Rail coal in her bag.

THE late grandmother of John McMenemy from Milngavie recalled that during World War II American soldiers stationed in Glasgow were bemused when the tram conductress would snap: "C'moan, getaff."

The mystified military men could never decide whether they were being ordered to stay or scram.

THE daughter of reader Gwen White attended university in London. Gwen was worried that she wouldn't embrace student life. A fear that was allayed when the teenager made her first phone call home after one week and without preamble said: "Mum, how do you get sick out of a coat?"

24

The Weird Stuff Keeps Weirdening

EILISH McColgan proved she's zippy on a running track by winning the 10,000 metre race at the 2022 Commonwealth Games in Birmingham, an event her mum, Liz, also won, over thirty years previously.

The Diary wasn't especially impressed. That's because Junior, the copy boy who works in our office, is just as fast as Eilish when he brings the staff their tea in the morning . . . and he happens to be ninety-eight years old. (The wizened old fellow has been with the Diary since the age of sixteen, and is still patiently waiting for his first promotion.)

How does Junior accelerate round the office with such speed and grace, you may wonder. The secret is that we permanently glued his feet to a skateboard, back in 1978. Now we just give him a hefty dunt, and away he screeches. (The noise is made by both his wheels and mouth.)

Of course, we never have to give our Diary contributors a hefty dunt.

Needing little encouragement – apart from the occasional gentle remonstrance with a hot poker – they happily supply us with a multitude of thrilling yarns, as you'll discover in the following chapter . . .

A LOGISTICAL thought from reader Ken Garner, who says: "The only thing fire drills teach people is how to sarcastically leave a building as a group."

GLASGOW taxi driver Mark Rushton gave a lift to an American tourist who said: "I love the simmering tension in your city. I was in the self-service queue at Sainsbury's and some drunk guy started screaming that he was being overcharged for Frosties. Felt like I was in a Vietnam movie."

OVERHEARD in a Newton Mearns coffee shop by reader Rebecca Townsend . . .

Elderly Lady Number 1: "Remember Albert?"

Elderly Lady Number 2: "Of course. Lovely man. Always so witty!"

Elderly Lady Number 1: "Well, yes. That's what I used to think. But he's just no fun anymore. I've bumped into him at loads of funerals, recently, and he's not cracked a smile once."

JET-SET reader Hamish Auld recalls being on a flight to Portugal and requesting a glass of water.

A cabin crew member replied: "Still?"

"Yup," said Hamish. "Haven't changed my mind in the last few seconds."

BACK in July the Edinburgh Festival hadn't even begun. Yet already the weird stuff was weirdening in Scotland's capital city.

In the Old Town's Bow Bar a knight of the realm entered the premises. And we don't mean a chap who sits in the Upper House of Parliament.

This was a noble fellow in a full suit of glittering armour, including helmet and visor. Thankfully he didn't bring a mighty steed.

Though he did waddle up to the bar. (It being almost impossible to swank or sashay up to a bar when fully garbed in clanking metal.)

A few words were muttered to the bartender, then he left.

This being Edinburgh, the staff and clientele were only mildly discombobulated.

Though comments were made about the mysterious warrior, with one tippler saying: "Bow allowing sportswear now?"

To which the management clarified: "Happy to make some exemptions. Rugby, tennis, elephant polo and jousting."

FEARS of a summer water shortage reminds Bryce Drummond from Kilmarnock of 1960s Edinburgh, when the city cut off H2O supplies for several hours each day, due to low reservoir levels.

After a recommendation was made for more reservoirs, one wise old resident protested that it was ridiculous to build new ones when there wasn't enough water in the existing ones.

SYMPATHETIC reader Jennifer Endfield points out: "A surprise party is the ultimate insult for a retiring detective."

THE Diary accepts that the local constabulary have a difficult job, though it can't be denied that they sometimes overstep the mark.

Reader Ted McLellan says: "A police officer stopped me due to the dilapidated state of my jumper sleeve, which is covered in small balls of thread."

Ted adds: "I've been charged with grievous bobbly arm."

MUSING on the wicked acts men sometimes perpetrate, reader Fred Donaldson says: "Arson is just crime brûlée."

AN English chap recalls visiting his aunt in Hamilton. Deciding to go fishing at Garrion Bridge, he asked a local which bus to take.

"You'll want the Biggar bus," he was helpfully informed.

Not realising there was such a location, the poor chap patiently waited on a double decker.

MUSIC fan Brian Murphy from Anniesland gets in touch to ask: "Which Scottish singer has the best vocabulary?"

The answer, apparently, is . . ."Gerry Synonym."

THE ageing process has some peculiar side-effects, notes Laura Shaw from Edinburgh. "I now have a favourite hob ring on the cooker," she says. "Back right. The Mr Darcy of hob rings. Never lets a girl down."

THINKING about growing older, Katherine Pearson from East Kilbride says: "If they ever discover the elixir of eternal youth, it should be marketed as the Neverage Beverage."

THE most prestigious night in the Diary's calendar is the Scottish NBL Awards, which took place in 2022 at Glasgow's Marriott Hotel.

As any civilised person will know, NBL stands for Nails,

Brows and Lashes, and the glamorous ceremony celebrates the creative geniuses working in the beauty industry.

Categories include "Lash Lift Specialist of the Year". (How do you lift a lash, we wonder. Does it involve a miniature winch attached to the side of the face?)

There's also a prize for the "Russian Lash Technician of the Year", which sounds like something a KGB interrogator could easily win . . .

SCOTLAND'S Festival for Science Fiction, Fantasy and Horror Writing, known as Cymera, took place in Edinburgh. With a bunch of writers from each of those quirky genres jetting in from around the world, it's no wonder that some highly eclectic conversations took place.

Texan sci-fi novelist Dale Thomas Vaughn certainly enjoyed the chinwaggery, saying: "Was out late at night in Edinburgh with authors and big thinkers, discussing topics like Kierkegaard, Irish history, Brazilian politics, the mathematical limit of text-to-speech, how to courier cats, and yes . . . sci-fi."

The Diary is glad the gang got round to sci-fi eventually. Though, quite frankly, all we want to hear about is how to courier cats.

ON Scottish social media one young lady, who has struggled with addiction issues, fondly recalls her grandmother, who died recently.

She says: "I keep thinking, at least my gran got to see me

sober. Then I think about how she didn't really understand the concept. When I told her I was eighteen months in recovery, she said: 'You deserve a brandy for that, hen.'"

THE Diary remembers with nostalgic fondness the genteel old days of the 1980s, when "doing the robot" was merely an innocent attempt at a dance move in Cleopatra's nightclub in Glasgow.

The phrase has now taken on more bawdy connotations, for we find ourselves reaching for the smelling salts upon being informed that humanised versions of robots, blonde of hair and blank of face, are to be sold as life-partners for the more desperate sort of male suitor.

These amorous automatons will be put to hard labour in the boudoir. More disturbingly, it seems they have been fitted with Glasgow accents.

Mechanically inclined reader David Donaldson says: "What I want to find out is does she say, 'Dae youse come here often?' And does she draw the line by saying, 'Gonnae no dae that?'"

SCIENTIFICALLY trained reader Bob Garnett says: "Did you know that candle flame smells like burnt nose hair?"

WORD reaches us that a cow – clearly seeking more thrills and high-adventure than can be experienced in your average meadow – was spotted on the Pollokshaws West train platform, contentedly licking his own reflection in the glass-fronted shelter. (Humans do this, too, occasionally.)

The folk at ScotRail have suggested that the migrating moo was probably waiting on the next train to Cowdenbeef.

DISTURBING news from Glasgow, where the Duke of Wellington statue outside the Gallery of Modern Art has been spotted without his traffic cone hat.

As you can imagine, the locals are not taking this desecration of a famous landmark lightly, and on social media a doom-laden prophesy is gloomily referenced: "If the Duke is unconed, no more tattie scones."

IT has been reported that burly builders are not bereft of a tender side. Research shows that many construction workers discuss their emotions with colleagues. They also enjoy literature and fine art.

This reminds David Donaldson of the chap with a pronounced Irish accent who applied for a job on a building site.

"What's the difference between a joist and a girder?" asked the foreman.

"Well," replied the applicant. "Joyce was an Irish author while Goethe was a German polymath."

HAVING discovered that robots with Glasgow accents have been built for use in the boudoir, we're now figuring out what these amorous automatons should be programmed to say. Russell Smith from Largs suggests: "Sorry. Nae the night. Power cut."

WE mentioned that Glasgow's iconic Duke of Wellington statue was spotted without his rightful adornment of a splendiferous traffic cone hat.

This has caused the traumatised citizens of the Dear Green Place to weep and wail like members of a Native American tribe whose totem pole has been burned to the ground.

Though one Glesga wag has managed to see the positive side of Welly without a traffic cone above his brow, writing on social media: "Does this mean it's okay to park up there now?"

25

Eejit, Eejit, Eejit, Eejit

A SHORT while ago the Diary mourned the death of dancer, choreographer and all round Mr Exuberance Lionel Blair, a chap who rose from ragged youth to razzle-dazzle old age.

Even in his nineties he refused to say sayonara to showbiz. If someone had offered him a pair of comfy slippers as a retirement gift, Lionel would have defiantly used them to perform an elegant soft-shoe shuffle.

The Diary is the journalistic equivalent of the late Mr Blair. Committed to light entertainment, we prefer to charm and disarm rather than alarm.

Sometimes the reporters in our department even wear top hats and tails while hunched over our desks. Such attire can be stuffy in the summer months, though we feel it adds a certain élan and joie de vivre to what we write. (And one day we fully intend on discovering what "élan" and "joie de vivre" mean. Which will really contribute to our prose style.)

The following chapter celebrates those who, like Lionel, died in the last few months.

Alas, none of them wore dancing shoes. Yet every single one of them exhibited the blithe bonhomie of the beatific Mr Blair . . .

ENGLISH comedian Sean Lock toured Scotland many times, and once revealed how a Dundee gig resulted in a moment of glorious triumph in a boozer.

Before a show at the city's Caird Hall in 2016 he visited a local museum and learned about the area, with the more important details being instantly memorised.

Years later there was a pub quiz that Sean took part in with friends, and a question was asked about Dundee.

"I didn't really listen to the question," revealed Sean, "but I told my mate to write down jute . . . and it ended up being right."

THE death of drummer Charlie Watts inspires the Diary to assess the impact of his band, The Rolling Stones.

Reader Jack McDaniel recalls trying to make new friends during Fresher's Week while attending Aberdeen University in the early 1980s.

He attempted to open a window into the soul of a fellow scholar at the student bar by enquiring if the bloke preferred The Beatles or Stones.

The chap merely shrugged and said: "Neither. At the moment I've *The Greatest Hits of the Bay City Rollers* on my turntable."

"That saved a lot of precious time," says our reader. "I hastily shuffled along the bar and never talked to that weirdo again."

MORE on Charlie Watts. Reader Melissa Bourke dated a bloke who adored jazz with as much passion as he despised rock music.

He once spotted a Rolling Stones album on a coffee table in Melissa's flat. The record had a picture of the band emblazoned across the front.

Pointing to each member of the Stones in turn, he made the following lofty pronouncement: "Eejit, eejit, eejit, eejit . . . nae bad oan the sticks."

FOOTBALLING icon Jimmy Greaves will be missed. Although he played for England, his greatest partnership was undoubtedly with Scotsman, Ian St John. The duo brought hilarity and hijinks to the beautiful game with their memorable TV show *Saint & Greavsie*.

Jimmy was always quick with a quality quip. He once said of former Rangers player, Paul Gascoigne, that he was: "A man capable of breaking both leg and wind at the same time."

WE continue reminiscing about Jimmy Greaves, who was always happy to share his astute thoughts about the game as it's played on the northern side of Hadrian's Wall.

Reader Pete Roberts remembers Jimmy saying of the fraternal bond between footy fans: "You'll never walk alone . . . unless you're a Hamilton Accies supporter."

FOOTBALL negotiations are normally fraught with tension. Battling participants parry over money and perks, while egos and agents ensure nothing runs smoothly.

When the late Walter Smith turned up at the gates of Paul Gascoigne's countryside gaff to try and entice him to Ibrox, things progressed slightly differently.

Paul was trundling along on a quad bike when he spotted Walter.

"Who is it?" said Gazza.

"It's Walter Smith," said Walter.

"What is it you're wantin'?" said Gazza.

"I'm here to see if you'll come to play for Rangers," said Walter.

"Aye, all right," said Gazza.

Then he gave Walter a piggyback on his quadbike, and they whizzed off to Gazza's house.

Job done.

NOWADAYS football is a glamorous game, highly lucrative for its practitioners. It was much the same when Bertie Auld played for Celtic in the 1960s. His first wage packet as a professional kickabout artist contained the grand sum of half a crown, roughly twelve pence in today's money.

Unfortunately he couldn't spend all of his vast wealth on fun and frolics. As Bertie once pointed out with a wry smile, being a professional footballer meant: "You had to buy yer ain boots."

WE'RE told the story of Bertie in later years, who was dining as a guest at Celtic Park, along with former teammate, Jimmy Johnstone.

Lamb chops were being served on the buffet table, and Jimmy, who was rather frail at the time, asked Bertie to bring him some.

Having enjoyed the food, Jimmy asked Bertie to fetch him more lamb chops.

A few minutes later the chef was seen dragging Bertie by the back of the neck from the kitchen.

"This is all your fault!" yelled Bertie to Jimmy, who asked why.

"I'm being done for chop lifting," said Bertie.

LORD Macfarlane was an illustrious fellow, sitting on the board of many top companies, and a keen patron of Scottish arts.

Reader Ron Cowley, like Lord Mac, was a member of Glasgow Arts Club. Ron once attempted to buy certain delicacies from the organisation's restaurant, but was informed that Lord Mac had already gobbled the goodies.

And did the tasty morsels in question include such aristocratic edibles as steak, truffles and caviar?

Not quite. The Lord had been munching Scotch pies, beans and chips.

WE mentioned above that Lord Macfarlane had simple tastes in cuisine.

Revd Dr Johnston McKay recalls dining next to him when he was Lord High Commissioner to the General Assembly.

After coffee had been served a waiter was observed approaching Lord Macfarlane with a chocolate bar on a salver.

A raised eyebrow brought the comment from the waiter: "His Grace enjoys a Yorkie at this time of night."

DUGLAS T. Stewart, lead singer with Bellshill band BMX Bandits, recalls meeting the late Stephen Sondheim on a TV programme.

Sondheim – who was often proclaimed as the greatest practitioner of musical theatre of his generation – was very complimentary about a Bandits love song that they played on the show.

The suave New Yorker was particularly enamoured by the ode's romantic title.

It was called . . . "Death & Destruction".

SONDHEIM, continued. Reader Brenda Lewis says: "He wasn't merely a lyrical genius. He could also forecast the future."

How so?

"Well," says Brenda. "Back in 1973 Sondheim predicted the rise of Boris Johnson and Nicola Sturgeon by writing 'Send in the Clowns.'"

GLASGOW guitarist Tam Harvey was a founding member of folk band The Humblebums, along with Billy Connolly. (Gerry Rafferty joined later.)

Though never finding the same level of success as his friends, Tam played an integral part in Scotland's music scene.

His daughter Georgiana Mannion tells us: "I grew up in a house where every folk musician worth their salt would come and stay. John Martyn, Hamish Imlach, The Fureys . . ."

None of these dignitaries impressed her quite so much as the time a supergroup of legendary status popped round.

Georgiana admits being especially dazzled during a visit by Alba's very own crack troupe of kiddie entertainers . . . The Singing Kettle.

THE death of Nobel Peace Prize winner Archbishop Desmond Tutu inspired many obituarists to focus, quite appropriately, on his fight against apartheid in South Africa.

Though John Mulholland noted with disappointment that there was no mention of the Archbishop's contribution to the rhyming slang of Glasgow.

"His name will surely live on amongst students," says John. "For those graduating from university with a lower Second Class Honours degree (abbreviated as 2:2) will forever refer to their qualification as a Desmond."

ANDY GORAM was, a truly inspirational cricketer for Scotland, also remembered for his aptitude between the sticks on the footy field.

What is less well known is that Andy had a sophisticated tactical knowledge when it came to the beautiful game.

He was once asked by the broadcaster David Tanner what style of play should be implemented by a new Rangers manager.

Andy's thoughtful reply was: "Just ****in' win."

A stratagem that is sadly often overlooked in the modern game.

THE Diary was sad to hear of the death of Nichelle Nichols, who played Lt Uhura in Star Trek. Reader Colin Williams met her at a signing in Glasgow's Forbidden Planet, and recalls listening to two sci-fi fans in front of him in the queue.

"This is like my own personal moon landing," enthused one chap.

"The moon's just a hunk of rubble in the sky," scoffed the other chap, who then added in a disappointingly sexist fashion: "If Neil Armstrong had landed on Uhura I'd have been a lot more impressed."

THE movie *Grease* was responsible for making an entire generation of British kids unhappy with their humble origins. (The editor of this book being one of them.) Where were our hot-rod cars? Our drive-in movies?

And why, when we studied the bathroom mirror, did we look nothing like Danny or Sandy?

The Diary was sad to hear of the death of Olivia Newton-John, who played Sandy with style and sizzle.

The popular singer and actress had an intriguing family tree. Her grandfather was a Nobel Prize winning physicist while her father was an MI5 officer working on the Enigma project at Bletchley Park.

She also had connections to Scotland, with sister Rona born in Edinburgh.

There was another claim to fame of a (slightly) Scottish nature.

Tartan troubadour Rod Stewart has admitted: "Her spandex trousers in *Grease* were my inspiration for my 'Do Ya Think I'm Sexy?' era."

Which is almost as historically important as a Nobel Prize winning grandad . . . though not quite.

The Queen . . . Some Memories

TIME for a shift in tone, folks. This was a sadly momentous year, for after a reign of more than seventy years, the Queen died in September.

We thought it appropriate to publish something slightly more sombre and reflective, starting with a quote from doom-n-gloomy Danish philosopher, Soren Kierkegaard. And it doesn't get more sombre and reflective than that . . .

O infinite majesty, even if you were not love, even if you were cold in your infinite majesty, I could not cease to love you. I need something majestic to love.

For many of her subjects, the late Queen Elizabeth provided a quiet comfort and reassurance, with her increasingly old-fashioned values of modesty, fortitude and dignity.

Our sovereign was also our solvent – the glue that kept all the disparate parts of the nation's psyche attached to each other.

Even those who hated everything the Queen stood for never seemed quite so British as they did when haranguing Her Majesty from afar. She brought out the doughty, grouchy, punk-rocky aspects of the nation's character.

The most ardent republican would probably agree that she provided a counterbalance to our increasingly loud, brash and self-centred age.

And what brave new world shall replace her generation?

Well, in future we'll receive all ethical guidance from Gary Lineker's tweets. And with every second church remodelled as a Wetherspoons, the holy spirit will arrive in shot glasses.

As bad as it's undoubtedly going to get there will always be memories from September 2022, when the Queen was laid to rest with all the dignified splendour that a beleaguered nation could muster.

Whilst admittedly such a highfalutin ceremony wasn't to everybody's taste, before the pomp and protocol, the British nation did what it invariably does best.

It queued.

Patiently, pragmatically, ponderously ... thousands stood in line on the streets of Edinburgh and London, waiting to bid farewell to their Queen as she lay in state in St Giles Cathedral and then Westminster Hall.

On the surface this was a celebration of monarchy. A triumph for the great, the grand, and the gilded. On a deeper level it was a fanfare for the common man and woman.

Thousands upon thousands came in search of their vanished Queen. And they found each other.

26

Zen out of Zen for Creativity

THE rage of the Scottish nation is legendary. We become "fizzin mad" when an English shopkeeper refuses to accept our money as legal tender. And we are "pure bealin" when our favourite tipple is spelt with an additional Irish "e" to become whiskey. (A parsimonious Scot would never be so profligate as to squander an unnecessary letter of the alphabet. We even manage to trim a few unwanted letters from another beloved refreshment, Irn-Bru.)

In May 2022, David Moyes, the Scottish manager of West Ham United, grumpily blootered a ball that proceeded to boing off a ball boy, proving once again that the argy-bargy Alba rabble have a fuse that is shorter than Danny DeVito in socks.

Thankfully steps have been taken to soothe the savagery that bubbles in the national breast. Labelled the "Cackle Cure", it's a panacea patented by the Diary, which we administer to both young and old, and everyone in between.

It's potent enough to make even the Incredible Hulk less belligerent, allowing him to take up a tranquil new hobby, such as croquet.

But how do we make our merry-making medicine, you may ask. Well, its concocted by our talented contributors, in the guise of the humorous lists, puzzles and poems that they often send us, in order to keep the nation entertained.

The following chapter samples a few of our favourites.

Enjoy . . .

* * *

THE Diary often worries that it is too entertaining for its own good. To counteract this bad habit, we decided to play a game where our readers describe their favourite movies in the most boring way possible.

(For the answers to the following, take a peek at the end of this chapter . . .)

1. Man and woman don't like each other, then like each other, then don't, then do.

2. Small people return stolen property.

3. Concerned step-parent encourages disobedient child to eat more fruit.

4. Pub owner bumps into ex-girlfriend.

5. Young chap joins family business and supervises period of growth in the firm.

6. Office worker takes much-needed motel break.

7. Scrappy chappie has daddy issues.

8. Boy makes new pal in the neighbourhood, goes on bike ride with him, then pal goes home to parents.

9. Little girl takes an afternoon nap.

10. Tradesman working in ironware and lead metal takes cash-in-hand for job.

11. TV weatherman goes on extended holiday.

12. Young girl breaks in new pair of shoes during lengthy stroll.

13. Chap does some digging in the back yard. Takes his time about it.

14. Writer struggles to complete first draft. Then succumbs to chilly draft.

15. Dodgy rich white supremacists fall in love.

* * *

MICHAEL GOVE, *who is perhaps the nation's most vivacious Conservative politician, was spotted gyrating in an Aberdeen nightclub.*

But which song enticed him onto the dance floor? Our inspired readers decided to guess . . .

JEFF Davidson suggests that Groovin' Gove was flailing his arms and legs around to a 1970s disco hit that celebrates the distinctive experience of being a Tory raised in Scotland.

"He must have been jigging to that Classic Chic song," says Jeff. "Le Freak."

MIKE Cagle concludes it was a classic Bob Dylan number, which Mad Moves Mike assumed was playing to celebrate his talent for delivering memorable speeches in the House of Commons.

That song is, of course . . . "Idiot Wind".

ANNA Atkinson says it was probably a song predicting the future glories of Gove's political career.

In other words, Paul Simon's "Slip, Slidin' Away".

RAB Henderson from Falkirk assumes it was the Mindbenders' "A Groovy Kind Of Love".

Though Rab says the version played in Aberdeen was no doubt A Groovy Kind Of Gove.

Or perhaps even A Govy Kind Of Groove.

WHEN he isn't gyrating with wild abandon, Gove has had many political posts, including being Chancellor of the Duchy of Lancaster. Which is why Stevie Campbell from Hamilton believes he must have been jiggling along to Musical Youth's 1980s anthem "Pass the Dutchie".

EVA Beveridge suggests it was a song celebrating Gove's two attempts to become Tory leader, when he came third, twice.

"Must have been that classic Beatles song," says our reader. "I'm A Loser."

DAVID Donaldson wants to know more about the name of the Aberdeen nightclub visited by Gove.

We hear rumours it's called Bohemia, though David thinks it should be Coconut Gove.

* * *

THE news that a stage musical version of Irvine Welsh's novel *Trainspotting* is planned has our readers musing about what songs to incorporate . . .

Robbie Franklin suggests adapting a classic lyric from *The Sound of Music* . . .

Raindrops on noses and whiskers of jakies,
Rusty auld needles, cheap lager from Aldi's,
White powder packages tied up with strings,
These are a few of my favourite things.

Malcolm Rourke suggests adapting lyrics from the musical *Oliver* ...

> Drugs, glorious drugs,
> We're pure daft aboot 'em,
> Overdosin' each day,
> Then coughin' up thick green phlegm,
> Just time tae stagger doon the buroo, nae workin' like mugs,
> Oh, drugs, wonderful drugs, marvellous drugs, glorious drugs ...

(P.S. Unlike the aforementioned songs, this book does not advocate the use of illegal substances. The only thing it's permissible to be addicted to is your yearly dose of Diary delirium.)

* * *

OUR meditative readers decide to compile a series of Zen teachings, which include the following ...

Always remember you're unique. Just like everyone else.

If you think nobody cares whether you're alive or dead, try missing a couple of mortgage payments.

Never test the depth of the water with both feet.

* * *

WE decided to build a Book Nook for our favourite scholarly works, as suggested by our readers. Here's our favourites . . .

The Role of Irony and Put-Downs in Scottish Literary Fiction by I. Thattleby-Wright

Ultra-Marathon Running in Ireland by Eamonn Payne

The Story of Bollywood Movies by brothers Dan and Roman Singh

American Gardening by Ida Hoe

Handbook for Hermits by Lisa Lane

Things Are Pretty Bad by Evan Elpus

The Best of Celtic Cooking by Iris Tew

* * *

THE Diary spotted a van in the Highlands which had the name Van Heilan written on the side, thus combining, for perhaps the first time, gnarly heavy metal music and picturesque Scottish scenery.

It also inspired us to come up with a few of our own names for vans . . .

Van Morrison (Used by a popular supermarket chain to deliver groceries.)

Martha and the Van Dwellers (Good name for a camper van.)

Van Rouge (For delivering wine.)

Van for the Road (Delivers all kinds of booze.)

Inspired by the vehicle named Van Rouge (see above), a reader argues that white, unmarked vans should be called Van Blanc.

Another reader suggests we extend our naming to tankers, giving us . . . Van Diesel.

A vehicle for delivering self-tanning and bronzing products could be named Van Tropez.

Garden furniture could be transported in a vehicle made ever so slightly sinister if it had written on its side . . . The Wicker Van.

With the rise in restaurants and takeaways delivering meals, a curry house could have written on the side of its delivery vehicle . . . Vandaloo.

A vehicle transporting sound engineers from one gig to another could be labelled . . . Van, 2, 3, Van, 2,3.

A vehicle for refuse collection could be named after a famous American soul singer . . . Van Dross.

Galleries could transport innovatory artwork in a vehicle with the words emblazoned across the side . . . A Van-Garde.

Preachers could spread the word of God, and also be eco-friendly, by driving electric vehicles emblazoned with . . . e-Vangelist.

A vehicle carrying cosmetics could be labelled Van . . . ity.

Television licence detector vans could have written on their sides: TV or not TV, that is the question.

A vehicle used in a mobile dry-stone walling business could be labelled Van Dykes.

* * *

AND finally, here's our answers to the fifteen classic films that we described in the most boring way possible at the beginning of this chapter . . .

1. When Harry Met Sally.
2. The Lord of the Rings trilogy.
3. Snow White and the Seven Dwarfs.
4. Casablanca.
5. The Godfather.
6. Psycho.
7. The Empire Strikes Back.
8. E.T.
9. Alice in Wonderland.
10. A Fistful of Dollars.
11. Groundhog Day.
12. The Wizard of Oz.
13. The Shawshank Redemption.
14. The Shining.
15. Gone with the Wind.

27
Verbose? Verboten

THE Labour Party has endured years of cock-up, chaos, crumble and Corbyn, resulting in the Red Wall looking like the nearby fortification built by Hadrian.

A few months ago the fightback commenced, with Keir Starmer writing a 14,000 word pamphlet laying out his plans for party and nation.

The only problem with a 14,000 word pamphlet is that it's a pamphlet. With 14,000 words.

Not many potential Labour voters were prepared to switch off Netflix, scrutinise the document, then say to their husband or wife: "Quick – get my magic marker! I want to underline paragraph 479, so I can repeat it down the pub. Won't my mates be impressed!"

Keir didn't realise that long-windedness is lethal, and only pithiness is perfection.

Which brings us to the following exceedingly short tales. Each one is sharp, succinct and sure to make you snigger.

Take heed, Mr Starmer.

MOVIE-LOVING reader Marvin Scott says: "Hollywood should announce a sequel to Groundhog Day, then release the original."

HISTORICALLY minded reader Alicia Hogan gets in touch to say: "Not many people know that the *Titanic* had a sister ship called the *Italic*. Luckily it didn't sink. It just leaned to one side."

"MY wife tells me I'm the cheapest person she's ever met," says reader Ken Robertson, "but I'm just not buying it."

HAVING decided to go on a diet, reader Julie Wright says: "I don't eat sandwiches, anymore. I quit cold turkey."

A MEDICAL vignette, provided by reader Oliver Carr:
   Doctor: I think you may be suffering from hypochondria.
   Patient (aghast): Oh no – not that as well!

"WHAT do you call a typo on a headstone?" asks reader Mary Shaw. "A grave mistake."

INQUISITIVE reader Martha Reid asks: "If you come second in a star naming competition do you get a constellation prize?"

AN irritated Gordon Redmond From Falkirk says: "I've just been moved to a different department in the prosthetics factory where I work, and it's really annoying. I'm up in arms."

"I WAS so shocked when my wife called me lazy when we were shopping," says reader Maurice Hare, "I nearly fell out of the supermarket trolley."

"I USED to be addicted to bath salts," admits reader Alan Scott. "But I'm clean now."

"BLACKBOARDS – they genuinely are remarkable," points out reader Matt Greig.

"MY friend keeps having nightmares about half eaten bananas," says reader Alan Smallwood. "Must be a mid-Fyffe crisis."

IRRITATED reader Mandy O'Dell says: "I feel like super-fluous has too many letters."

"IF I could be any superhero, I'd be Aluminium Man," says reader Ted Merton. "My superpower would be foiling crime."

A SACRILEGIOUS observation from reader Albert Taylor, who points out that Holy Water isn't used in vaccines because you can't take the Lord's name in vein.

GREEN-FINGERED reader Julia Wilson has been trying to grow genetically modified apples. "But now it's all gone pear-shaped," she sighs.

LINGUISTICALLY limber reader Mike Peake explains to us the definition of "jousting".
   "It's what a Brummie asks a bee," says Mike.

CURIOUS reader Edward McGuire gets in touch to ask: "If I accidentally rub ketchup in my eyes does that give me Heinzsight?"

"I MET my wife on the net," says reader Robert Deane. "We were both rubbish on the trapeze."

HISTORICALLY minded reader Michelle Cornwell gets in touch to explain: "If a castle is downgraded to a fort, you could say that it's been de-moated."

"MY wife recently called me pretentious," says reader Oliver Thompson. "I was so surprised my monocle fell out."

FASHION conscious Chris Ide from Waterfoot says: "I used to have a smoking jacket until it went on fire. Now it's a blazer."

"MY wife and I watched two films, back-to-back," says reader Alan Bullimore. "Luckily I was the one facing the TV."

MANY people struggle with modern technology, and reader Mandy Simms is no different. "I tried to send Bugs Bunny a file through Google Drive," she says. "But he only accepts a WhatsApp doc."

* * *

Alas, we must now wish our readers a fond adieu until next year.

For it's time to quote that rapscallion rabbit mentioned in the above tale, as the Diary team takes an exhausted bow, and says to each and every one of you . . .

That's All, Folks!